Fire to Light

Charles Malone

FIRE TO LIGHT

FIRE TO LIGHT

A Memoir of Family, Race, and War

Paramount Press

Paramount Education,
P.O. Box 1150
Washington D.C. 20009

A cooperative approach to the humanities and social sciences through education, research, and writing.

Cover Design by Demarcus Williams
FRESHDESIGNZ, LLC

ISBN: 069282121X
ISBN-13: 978-0692821213

FOR DONNA

1

I settled into my seat for the long flight, tightened the seat belt and took a deep breath, as the powerful engines thrust the old jet airliner into the night, the surge of the lift off felt like rocks lying on my chest and castanets ringing in my ears.

I could see only the dark silhouettes of human shapes in the seats around me. Nobody said a word. Once we cleared the airport lights, it was dark everywhere, except for a blinking red light above the cockpit door up front. The rush was abated in an instance once airborne, the sensation of drag racing on the ground replaced by a buoyancy, as if we were birds suddenly in flight.

The passengers around me were not exactly strangers, but almost. We were all heading for the same destination, but what we would have to do, or whether we would stay together, was still an unknown. I didn't have a friend among them, so I kept to myself. I was there more in body, than in spirit. My attitude was still a work in progress. But it was time, at last, to deal with my reality, not to waste time wishing I was somewhere else. Many of the other guys on this flight were as unsettled as me, if the truth be known.

Thankfully, I had a window seat and nobody sitting next to me. Few of the passengers were pairing up, so my desire to be alone was commonplace. All of us were lost in our thoughts for a long while. But soon enough, some guy laughed at a joke, and then I heard somebody coughing behind me. We had time on our hands, even if shrouded by the fog of fear, and we were not going to stay quiet forever.

I began to snooze, went out for a while, but jolted back to life when we hit a little turbulence. *Whoa, what was that?* I thought. Nervous laughter emitted behind me. I turned around and saw a young man, wide-eyed in fear, looking at me as if I could save him from the quandary at hand.

"You okay, buddy?" I asked.

"Yeah, but don't like flying," he said.

"Too late now, don't you think?"

"I know. I know."

"Hang in there, buddy."

The kid still looked scared, but he managed a faint smile. I nodded my head to him, as if to say we were being threatened, but not under attack. This seemed to settle things between us. I had a knack for calming the younger ones, as most were, with my generally reflective view of life. If they got into the moment too much, I didn't get into it enough. We both returned to our reveries.

I didn't have any luggage on me. Our bags were loaded in storage below somewhere in the belly of the plane, a 707 American Boeing jet airliner. With a small cadre of female flight attendants on board, our flight seemed ordinary on the surface. As the hours passed, some of the guys perked up, made more noise, and teased the flight attendants, who had heard it all before and behaved accordingly. Growing restless, I cut on the light and tried to read a magazine. But it was hard to concentrate apart from the surreal reality of this airplane ride to parts unknown. I flipped through a few pages, gave up, and put the magazine down.

I began to think of home, my past in general. My life history was as twisted as anybody else, I supposed. I'd suffered my share of ups and downs. I had grown up in a small, rural town in the American south, where our family, while not impoverished, was somewhere between working class and middle class, but who really admits to their actual class standing? My mother thought we were practically upper class, but that is another story. My bone-weary dad knew differently. We were expected to do our chores, even though we were town kids and not strictly of the farm. I knew what it was like to soil my hands from work, for I hired out in the summers to tobacco and cotton farmers to help harvest their crops.

At home, we had little extra money. I was used to sharing with my two older brothers, everything from food portions to hand-me-down clothes to the single bathroom in our little box house. The saving grace for us was when we looked around at our neighbors, their lot in life looked the same as ours, many were worse.

Yet, aside from the usual family strife and small town trifling, we were content in our small world. My boyhood coincided with the serene 1950s, the Eisenhower years, complete with Davy Crockett hats, hula hoops and tinker toys. We mostly played neighborhood football, basketball and baseball on open land we had to hack down with sling blades in order to make the rocky, weed-choked fields playable. When alone, I favored filling my time playing with clay figures. I liked to put my imagination to work. If there was no way, we made a way.

My thoughts shifted back to our ongoing flight. I was not improving my mood by repeatedly thinking of home. It had been only a few hours since I placed last minute calls to them to give my farewells to my family at the Oakland holding station. It seemed like ages. I watched more clouds race by as the flight continued. I was hoping at this point that the old Boeing 707 we were on would make it safety to the first leg of our long journey: Anchorage, Alaska.

Our plane hit a little turbulence and then leveled off. After a little cursing, joking and settling in, we became quiet. We just got through it, not excited to get to the snowy stopover awaiting us. We landed around 3 o'clock in the morning. When I walked down the gangplank, I could see nothing but a black sky above and white snow around me. The dark sky had remnants of the northern lights. We stared in wonder at the banners of red, green and purple that illuminated the black sky. It was eerily quiet. The airport was ghostly looking, shrouded in a misty fog.

The airport inside was bleak, reflecting the remote, cold arctic night outside. Surprisingly, the restaurant was open. A lone waitress served up something to eat. I had apple pie, a surprise touch of home. We were quiet mostly. Most of us were anxious about our next take off because we knew it could be the perilous flight of our lives.

After a while, we heard the call to file outside and get ready to board the plane. I took my plate and glass to the counter.

"See you later," I said.

"Bye now," the waitress said with a slight smile. She looked really tired.

"Thanks. Good apple pie."

"The least we could do, honey."

I smiled and got in line to leave. I doubted I'd see the likes of this nice, homely lady again for a long time.

Once outside the airport cafeteria, we sat around a while longer, some of us wandering out into the snow to stare some more at the miraculous colors in the Alaskan sky. It was deeply cold, however, so we were almost glad to board the plane, fueled and ready to go, for the next leg of our journey.

Someone told us it was time to go.

"Good-bye, USA!" the kid cried out.

"Don't sound so cheerful about it, fool," a grumpy looking kid said, obviously an unwilling participant in our wandering party.

The route we took had us soaring in a broad arch over the Aleutian Islands in the northern Pacific Ocean, part of which was near the Russian and Chinese borders. I'd never felt more vulnerable to a ghastly death than in that flight, knowing we had no chance to survive a crash in this remote, fierce area of the world. We settled in for the long flight. We had been apprehensive prior to our arrival in Alaska, but the second leg of the journey over sea waters in total darkness gave us a sense of unshakable foreboding. We set in for a very long haul. We had guys talking some, laughing here and there, but again a silence fell over us for most of the many hours we were in route to our final destination.

As we continued to drone along in the night, my mind drifted back to my hometown. I found myself missing those tranquil days, even the good folk I used to think of as dullards. I recalled standing around the glowing potbelly stove at the local grocery store near our house, chewing the fat with the old farmers, or the country women, usually busier knitting or shelling peas than joining in the man talk. If kids my age were there, they had been wistful, like me, dreaming of being somewhere else, not huddled near that cast-iron stove listening to the same old stories and lies from their elders.

Well, we got our wish, I thought to myself with a chuckle, for I certainly was somewhere else now, and then some. My mind snapped back to my surroundings.

I'm not scared that much. I just don't want to be here, so that trumps everything else. It's stupid, after all. I'd never been selfish to a fault, I felt. I knew life was not just about me; or did I?

At long last, we were alerted to sit up, gather the gear we had, and strap in for landing. Peering out of my window as we descended several hundred feet above ground level, the first sight I could make out was a large rice field, a few water buffalo, and a little man, knee-deep in watery rice patties, clad in black pajamas and wearing a conical straw hat. Bending over as he did his work, he never looked up as we swooped over him.

Once on the ground, we lined up with our small bundle of belongings, and made for the forward exit. I said good-bye to the friendly flight attendants. Then as

I left the plane and began the descent down the steps, the 100 plus degree heat hit me like a blast from an open furnace. The sky was bright and all I could see was flat, clay ground. There were scores of us milling around amid scattered vans and trucks and jeeps parked all over the place. I continued down the steps. I noticed there was razor wire spread around, as well, like you seen atop prison walls. Beyond the wire, across the vast terra cotta fields, there was a long, blackish garland of trees in the distance. I skipped the last step and jumped to the dusty ground and raised a cloud around my legs.

My God, I'm in South Vietnam.

2

I was both thrilled and petrified at the same time. It was surreal, and I walked over to a set of bleachers with my compatriots to await further instructions. We sat there, still not saying much, trying to adjust from leaving an air-conditioned plane to the oppressive, tropical heat that now engulfed us. We were also quickly scanning the distant tree line of silky oaks looking for incoming mortars. Oh, how quickly I, the reluctant draftee, was shedding my intellectual qualms about the war and was replacing them with a survival instinct that would have made my mad dog drill sergeants proud.

To ease my discomfort, I popped on a cassette tape I had in my handheld cassette player and listened to a softly played "Carolina in My Mind" by James Taylor.

His soft words of home put me in an easy frame of mind, connecting me to my home state and country, even as I sat there on the other side of the world.

Within an hour or so we were moved to nearby Long Binh Post, a sprawling U. S. Army logistics base. This was the home of the U. S. Army Vietnam HQ Command (USARV) and the largest U. S. Army base with over 50,000 American troops. This was the dispersing point for all incoming and outgoing troops. We would know our fate soon enough, but for now we were going to cool our heels for a few days. It was a crowded place, with all kinds of people rushing around, both American and Vietnamese. I soon enough had to relieve myself in an open trench, peeing into the soft mud, while trying not to gag from the stench.

That night I lay there on my wet iron mattress and let my mind drift back to how I had managed to get drafted into the Army in the first place. *Stupid me*, I thought, *stupid me*.

It began when I let my grades lapse while in college. I was riding high as a summer staff member on Capitol Hill in Washington, D.C., loving the Georgetown nightlife, concerts, girls and the political fare in the halls of Congress. I had been appointed for summer duty by the Office of Senator Sam Ervin of North Carolina, mainly by the efforts of his administrative assistant, Jack Spain, an old political war horse, who had taken a liking to me. I was lucky to be there and was working there for the third summer in a row in 1970. I knew in my heart-of-hearts that I should have stayed in summer school back home to get my grades up, but my desire to satisfy my taste for instant gratification won out over prudence.

The moment of academic truth finally caught up with me. College officials summoned me home from Washington and strongly advised that I should take some courses during the last semester of summer school in order to make "satisfactory" progress in my academic schedule. There was a veiled academic threat behind the advice, so I took heed, gave notice in Washington, and returned home in time to register for the second session of summer school.

I tried to do well, although I was in a huff about it all, and did pass the two courses I took. It was tough being home after being in the midst of the big city energy of Washington, D.C. I also knew there was to be a resurrection of the draft lottery in December. I needed to stay in college to be exempt from the lottery, which would conscript young men into the military who were considered I-A, which meant being eligible for the draft.

Staying in college was a popular way to avoid the draft. I am ashamed to say I was not giving much thought to most of the young men in America, certainly in North Carolina, who were not in college. I was just thinking of myself. I thought I was okay, even if I got a low lottery number since I would likely be back in school in the fall.

But I knew there was a possibility I could be drafted. A draft lottery drawing - the first since 1942 - was going to be held in December, at Selective Service National Headquarters in Washington, D.C. This event would determine the order of call for induction during calendar year 1970. I was in the eligible age groups.

Nonetheless, I was getting ready for the fall semester. I had a couple of free weeks before classes would begin. Then I got a call from the college registrar's office asking me to come in and meet with the head registrar, known as Colonel Harris. This guy was ex-military and scary. He always went by the book and in handing out decisions, took no prisoners. But I wasn't too nervous; after all, I had complied with what the school wanted and returned home that summer. And I had passed the two courses I took.

I went to the registrar's office at the appointed time. I was escorted in by the secretary and greeted Colonel Harris. We shook hands, which became a grip off exchange. I rubbed my hand after I sat down, so he couldn't see. A foreboding feeling came over me. I was now feeling a bit nervous. The Colonel sat back down, and then he began to gaze at me, as he slowly drew deeply on his cigarette. He leaned back a little in his executive chair, slowly exhaling the smoke. And he continued to gaze at me. I was thinking: *what the heck is he waiting for?*

"Charles, I have the results of your summer grades," he said suddenly, now leaning in some. He was still unsmiling.

"Yes, Colonel. I made a special effort to return from Washington to take the classes."

"That was considerate of you, Charles. It was what we wanted you to do. It was what you had to do, really."

"Yes, Colonel. I'm glad I passed them both."

"That's right, Charles, you passed them both. But your quality point average was not improved by making two Cs. The object of the summer assignment was to improve your grade point average."

"Well, that is the ultimate goal. Of course," I said weakly. I was beginning to sweat now.

He looked at me with a sour expression and leaned in some more. He spoke again with a hard edge to his voice.

"You didn't improve anything. You have dragged along all last year, passing everything, but not moving ahead—at all!"

"I know, Colonel, but I'm going to do better, I swear," I said. Now, I was scared out of my wits.

"Well, I won't prolong this, young man. I think you need to learn what you do has consequences. You need to mature. And to do so, I believe you need to sit out this fall and think over just how you want to approach your obligations as a student."

"Sit out? You mean I can't come back for the fall semester?" I was bewildered.

"Yes, you must sit out this fall. You've had more than enough chances to make some headway in your grades. You need to think it over. You are eligible to return for the spring semester that begins in January 1970. That is all, you can go now."

"Yes, sir," I said, standing to leave.

The Colonel stood and shook hands with me. I gave him a hard look. He returned my look with a set expression of his own. He slowly sat back down in his chair, leaned back while inhaling again on his cigarette. He was ready for me to get out of there.

I left and walked out onto the courtyard area, where all the students walked to and fro to their classes. My mind was racing, but I was also beginning to get mad. First of all, I couldn't believe the school was turning down any opportunity to get tuition fees from any guy or gal not mentally defective, much less from somebody who had never failed a course there in two years.

Just because I was not making sufficient progress? I thought. It didn't occur to me that Colonel Harris had hit the nail on the head in his summary of my academic standing. He also had told the hard truth about my attitude, which was that of a young man performing in a static way, not down or up, and showing no sign of improvement.

At this exact moment, I was a walking and talking example of a petulant young man, who had never had the strengthening influence of a father. I did not understand tough love. I had always known only unconditional love from home, whether it was for my good or not. I was getting tough love now, whether I liked it or not.

I may have gotten what I deserved, technically, but I could not see anything positive in the decision. I was on fire with rage. To my mind, this old goat had just made me eligible for the military draft, because I was now I-A. I was still blind to the truth that my suffering was self-inflicted. What I did see was that I would now have the pleasure of having my name entered in the forthcoming December 1 military lottery. I had expected to avoid being affected by the lottery because I would be in college. I had no doubt this little Napoleon knew I would become I-A if I had to drop out. I could not imagine how the old man would think I needed a military experience to ever grow up. I hated Colonel Harris at that moment like I had never hated anybody in my life.

But, after I cooled down a bit, I began to hate myself even more. I had put myself into this situation, always fluffing off my homework, dropping classes, going to DC to get my political fix, and just, hell, anything I took a fancy to do over my job as a student.

I was livid at the world for there being a war going on and livid at myself for being stupid enough to get myself eligible to be drafted into military service.

That first night I awoke in my bed, a metal frame thing with no mattress. My bottom and feet were soaked from the monsoon that had poured water across the dirt floor inside our tent in the middle of the night. The wet brought out an army of mosquitoes. *Well, OK,* I thought, *looks like this won't be like the Holiday Inn back home.* It is amazing how much we can endure with some aplomb when we see everybody else suffering the same way. All the guys were listening to their radios or cassette players, playing cards, yelling and cursing, or just moving around. We were still in limbo stuck in this waystation before we would be assigned somewhere "out there." All we could do was let off steam.

3

After a couple of days becoming oriented in Long Binh, the day of reckoning arrived. I figured we were heading for a duty location near water, being we were river boat people. But our plans were interrupted by a change in priorities by the high command.

"Listen up, people," said the captain at a meeting for our boat group. "You soldiers over here for river boat duty will have some options, as of today. Due to recent orders from command, we're handing over patrol duty on the rivers to the Vietnamese. This is a work in progress, but we'll be totally out of it in a few months. This is the policy of "Vietnamization" I am told. It means for you guys you have a choice: you can go river boat for a short while, or transfer to another duty right now."

"Ain't this a crock," one of the guys said from behind. We all started to chatter about what to do. Looking around we could see sign posts designating where we could go, ranging from relatively safe areas, such as Saigon, to hell holes up north, such as Quang Tri, Pleiku, and Da Nang.

The captain went on to say we were coming into Vietnam at a time of transition, when formerly American responsibilities were now being transferred to the Vietnamese. He said we were still engaged in a war, were under fire, but we were not seeking out the enemy as before. "Cover your own ass, guys. That's my advice," the captain said, as he dismissed us. With that parting shot, the captain destroyed any fighting spirit we might have had. Our little group gathered outside the briefing area to figure out what to do.

I didn't know what to think, at first. The option of bypassing river boat duty was a shocking new development. I had mixed feelings because I had fiercely opposed my assignment to river boat duty, but had warmed to it, especially after bonding with the guys. Still, it remained dangerous duty with no clear objective. I could only blame myself for ending up here. My insolence back at military police school at Fort Gordon had probably sealed my fate, via a revengeful sergeant. I could see now how it all led to my adventures in San Francisco and at Mare Island, home to the river boat patrol training school.

My duty orders out of Basic Training at Fort Polk, Louisiana, were to report to Fort Gordon, Georgia, for military police training. I had avoided the dreaded advanced infantry training, which was held in the northern section of Fort Polk, called "Tiger Land." I was relieved and ready to go. It was a happy plane ride in the night to Georgia. It had been a long five months in Louisiana, cut off from home, no television, no North Carolina newspapers, and little word from home, except for a few letters.

Fort Gordon, formerly known as Camp Gordon, was established in 1917. It housed the U. S. Army Signal Corps and "The Provost Marshal General School," i.e., Military Police. The fort is located in Augusta, Georgia. Military Police School was not as intense as basic had been. This training program was set up to teach us specific things about military police work, not to make us soldiers per se. We had already proven we were soldiers because we had graduated from basic training, so in this regard, our daily routines were disciplined without being as punishing and harassing as before.

By now, it was deep in November and cold, cold, cold. We were advised to purchase some long johns, which were thermal underwear with long sleeves and long pants. It was made from cotton back then. Well, it only took one morning of freezing to death for a long, long time while standing at attention as we waited to enter the mess hall for breakfast, sans the long johns, to learn I needed to run as fast as I could to buy them. I had to give these guys a nod for knowing practical things I didn't know. They had been trying to help me, but I was foolish in my resistance to getting help from "lifers."

Despite myself, I found MP School interesting overall. We had classes on rules of evidence and on how to arrest people, how to execute raids, surveillance, traffic safety, baton use as a weapon, and driving a jeep on patrol duty. It was a good mix of inside and outside training. I respected the Army attitude that as military police we had a duty to use our batons—wooden sticks—sensibly. An instructor told us that if we were in a bar brawl, we would mostly likely be the only person there under control. We had a duty to use the baton as a weapon to disable, not kill people. We were shown how to hit people in the places, such as on the shin, rather than the head, to bring them down. We were expected to keep our head precisely because the crowd would not. I have never had patience with police gone wild ever since. They have the power— no need to flaunt it. But my obstinacy to being told what to do got me in trouble once again. In this instance, I was not being simply willful. I felt I had a valid point in refusing to do what my company sergeant wanted me to do.

The company sergeant was tasked with getting all the MP recruits to subscribe to an MP magazine. Pretty simple, really. We were to sign up and have a small amount taken out of our paycheck to get the monthly magazine. Everyone signed up but me. I refused to go along. I told the sergeant that I was a draftee. Not sure, now, why I thought this self-disclosure helped my case. And I announced I would comply with all lawful orders, but not unlawful ones, like being told to subscribe to, what in effect, a trade magazine. I told him it was a form of unionization and I didn't have to do it. I stood my ground.

At first, the sergeant was mildly disappointed, but let it go. But after several weeks with me still holding out, he turned up the pressure. I found myself assigned, inordinately it seemed to me, to clean out offices and do extra policing of outside areas. I was once singled out for no apparent reason and made to crawl over gravel to pick up trash. All the while, other soldiers continued to walk in a line to police the same area. I was being picked on, but couldn't prove it. In my mind, simply being in the Army was imposing enough on me; I didn't have to agree to superfluous things that were not crucial to my work.

In retrospect, this little rebellion may have seemed stupid, but everybody ought to have a conscience-driven limit to what they will compromise on. I had reached mine. This demand just didn't set well with me. So, despite various threats from my superiors, I refused to budge. I was certainly threatened with being recycled, but I knew the magazine sign-up initiative was off the wall. Everyone else thought it was unnecessary, but to get along, they choose to go along.

Why was I so obstinate? Coming off three summers on Capitol Hill working for Senator Sam Ervin, a noted defender of the rights of citizens against the coercion of government, perhaps to a fault, had probably influenced me to resist Uncle Sam. For Senator Ervin, most expansions of federal power were a blueprint for a police state. I didn't always agree with the senator on the application of these ideals, especially on civil rights for minorities, but I thought his philosophy fit the bill concerning my dispute over the military police magazine dues requirement.

I wasn't trying to be simply headstrong, as much as I was trying to be true to a principle of personal freedom. I thought I'd given up enough freedom by accepting my draft notice and not running away, or letting myself go to jail. Enough was enough. I was guilty of self-serving, immature behavior on many things, in the Army and before, but I believe I was motived by higher motives on this question. However, my superiors got the last laugh. I found out the sergeant in charge of our squad got extra time off and a cash bonus if he got one-hundred percent of the trainees under his command to sign up for the MP magazine. I ruined that sweetheart deal by not signing up. He did not get his bonus because of me. It was probably that simple. He was determined to get back at me. In his mind, I had it coming for blocking him from getting his just rewards for the magazine recruitment. This payback had nothing to do with the Army mission, or anything material to our essential training.

I got my comeuppance this way. Our MP class of 150 graduated in February of 1971: about 80 went to Germany, about 62 went to West Point, and the remaining eight, including me, were sent to Vietnam, via California. The lucky eight were to go first to Riverboat Patrol School in Mare Island, California, and following that training, go straight to the rivers of South Vietnam.

On the day when our assignments were printed on a bulletin board, my name was absent. Everybody was abuzz over their assignments, especially the fortunate ones going to Germany. There were no direct Vietnam assignments, so I thought I was okay there, but where was my name? I'd forgotten about the river boat possibility. We had had a meet up several weeks before and the drill sergeant had asked for volunteers for river boat duty, since it was so dangerous. The river boat training was under the direction of the Navy, but Army MPs were assigned to it since they were considered sentry, and a significant part of the tasks assigned to this particular boat, the River Patrol Boat (RPB), was guard duty for barges and supplies, or personnel, going up and down the interior rivers and coast of South Vietnam. Only a handful of guys had signed up. We had heard the mortality rate for this duty was among the worst, so it did not have much appeal in the waning days of the conflict. I say waning, but we were still losing around fifty American soldiers weekly in Vietnam. Yet, our reduced involvement was still dangerous, and that meant until the very last hour, the risks were real for anyone over there, regardless of what they were doing, or where they were located. Everywhere was a front line in Vietnam, we'd been told. But later in the day, the few trainees whose names had not appeared with the initial lists were posted. My name was there.

We were assigned to the same place and same duty: River Patrol Boat duty in Mare Island, California. I was stunned. I remember having to do jeep patrol within a few minutes after reading my name on the list. I was driving a jeep by myself, just going around the post, my eyes filled with tears. I wasn't being brave at that initial hour. But by that evening, as we all sat around talking about our assignments, I was doing all right. I was actually enjoying the special attention directed at me, especially from the jealous gung-ho boys. One of the guys, a real Rambo, was working up his anger over not being assigned to river boat.

"Hell, man. How come a college boy like you is going to Nam and on river boats, to boot? I want to kick some Viet Cong ass and I've got to go to West Point and do nothing but kiss the brass's ass, and do spit and polish all day," he said.

"I'm sorry, Jesse. I'd be happy to change with you. But what can I do?" I said with a wry smile on my face.

"I don't know, but it ain't fair. I wanna fight, not be a toy soldier at a damn military academy."

The next day I heard that Jesse and a few of his buddies went to the Command Sergeant Major asking to him to switch our orders, but the chief threw them out. I had not objected to them going to make their plea, but I knew it would come to nothing.

So, while I was enjoying my special status with my buddies, I knew inside that I was in trouble. What lay ahead for me was no joke. I knew the fun and games were over. I had to reach down deep and figure how to face this new challenge.

Since five guys had volunteered for this extremely dangerous duty, that left only three to be picked at random, including me. Naïve, I hadn't yet figured out that I'd been screwed over. I still thought it was blind bad luck. A few months later, I connected the dots. I suddenly understood it, like a light bulb coming on in my head. The revelation came to me, actually, while I was sitting around with my new river boat patrol trainees, most of them wannabe hippies, in our barrack in California, griping about Army life in general. I recall a guy had a cassette of Crosby, Stills, Nash and Young blaring away in the background. I grimaced at first at the thought of how foolish I'd been. I grinned a little, too, because I had to admit: *that the old sergeant got me good*.

I had been had, I finally knew. And I had asked for it, really. Had I been brave, or foolish? Probably both. I was warned to go with the flow, but I willfully resisted to the end. The sergeant had been true to his word when he told me one evening, after he had failed to turn me, "Okay, Malone, have it your way. But know this, son: you are the grass; I am the lawnmower."

Yeah, I had been warned, and I had been too blind to see it coming. Still, even after I had figured it out, I never regretted my decision.

I left Fort Gordon for California and was met with a stunning aerial view: San Francisco. The plane was now descending on this popular West Coast city and beginning a circling pattern. If the California coastline had enamored me, I was mesmerized by the sight of this magnificent city with its skyscrapers standing tall on the edge of a peninsula jutting out from the mainland to the south. The Bay Area was vivid with its sparkling, blue water, forming a vast natural harbor. The iconic Golden Gate Bridge, a brilliant man-made structure, was clearly a distinctive link between San Francisco and Oakland, a huge city in its own right. I also noticed Alcatraz Island, home of the infamous, but now abandoned, prison, standing in solemn isolation in the bay. I felt a little like a prisoner myself, but I was being petulant, still at odds with being a non-civilian in the midst of a civilian play land.

The plane made a smooth landing, and I got through customs without difficulty at the huge, busy airport. After fending off a couple of panhandlers, I found a cab and was driven with wild abandon to my reporting site at Fort Presidio.

I was in uniform when I got there, so I was immediately pushed back in the military world once I got through the gate at Presidio. I was plunged into the odious duty of processing in. This fort was temporary quarters before I was to be transferred to nearby Mare Island, upstream about twenty miles, and home to the River Boat Patrol training program.

Presidio was by far the most handsome Army post I'd ever seen. My quarters on Montgomery Street were part of a series of red brick barracks, topped with red clay tile roofs and inviting white painted front porches. The post restaurant I frequented a lot had a view to kill for: the Golden Gate Bridge on the left and the island of Alcatraz on the right. The Bay, as we called it, was the magnificent backdrop for this panoramic scene. And if this beauty was not enough, the weather was divine. As a son of the South, I was used to a lot of humidity, but there was little of it here. Breezy, mild weather prevailed no matter where I traveled, even within the city where tall buildings intervened between the waters and me.

But I was getting lonesome soon enough. I actually endured a painful little U.S.O. dance one night. A turntable playing 45 Rpm records provided the music. The kind lady chaperons had refreshments and drinks available for free, and if there hadn't been ten soldiers to every one woman there, it might have been an agreeable social scene. Everybody was smoking cigarettes, as was the custom in those days, making the basement room foggy to the eye and acrid to the nose. The scratchy pop tunes playing off the vinyl had little appeal to me, so I soon said my good-byes and walked slowly back to my quarters.

I couldn't help but think of my father, who had written home during World War II, describing how he was languishing in a Y.M.C.A. hotel in downtown San Francisco, listening to the Guy Lombardo Orchestra on the radio playing "Marie." Later that evening, I was listening to the Carpenters perform "Close to You," on the radio, in a similar way, alone, and as lonesome as he must have been those many years ago.

At least he had a wife, I thought, while I had never had a long-term girlfriend. I was writing to a girl I'd recently dated back home, just a few months before I was inducted into the Army. She was a classy thing, daughter to a former federal judge and gubernatorial candidate, and I was the poor guy several rungs down the social ladder, so all the initiatives were mine. She would write to me on occasion, just answering me, of course. To be fair, she didn't know me that well, and no promises had been made. I should have quit writing her, but I was a heartsick soldier away from home. I was willing to be humble just to get a letter from a girl, no matter how I managed it.

Soon enough I arrived at my duty station where the rubber would meet the road: Mare Island. It was home to the U. S. Navy's repair facilities, mothballing operations, submarine operations, and riverine training operations for Swift Boats (larger with more firepower) and River Patrol Boats.

The atmosphere at Mare Island was not as severe as what I'd become accustomed to at my previous stops in Louisiana and Georgia. It was run by the Navy, after all. The food was better, the buildings newer, the grounds prettier and there was beautiful, blue water all around. Also, the discipline was relaxed. The guys in the Navy actually had cool bellbottom jeans and could keep their hair long and have beards. Jeez! I couldn't believe it. None of us Army guys got a haircut the whole time we were there, enjoying this new freedom. We were too timid to grow a beard, however. I was beginning to enjoy myself, despite myself. Even more, my attitude by this time, concerning my willingness to train and be in the mode of a soldier, was going through a slow, but perceptible, change. During Basic and MP school, I'd been reluctant to embrace anything the Army was teaching me as something sensible to know. My own bias against the military, which was not universal and was more a push-back against being drafted, had been poisoning my reasoning.

Yet, I had enough common sense to learn fundamental things during my military training because I knew I might need the knowledge to survive one day. Still, I'd resisted learning beyond what I thought was necessary, regardless of the subject matter. By the time I got to military police school, I was growing less belligerent, despite my spat over the magazine subscription. I was rebelling there on a question of principle, and I still did not regret that decision, fatal as it had turned out to be for me.

But now, in this unique school taught by the Navy, so different from what I ever suspected to be in, I recognized the value of the training with a greater acuity than I had ever felt before. I was more receptive to being a team player by now, and I had developed an acute feeling of not wanting to let my compatriots down. The old military adage: "Ours is to do or die, not to reason why," actually rings true in the real world of soldering. But the adage is true due to soldiers looking out for each other, not from a brute obedience to authority.

Although there was a sunny ambiance to the Mare Island facility that left the Army atmosphere in the dust, the actual river patrol boat training was serious. We soon began a busy schedule both in class and in the field. In the field, this time, meant either piloting the boats over water, or fixing them while at bay. We had to learn the how and why of the engines, communications, and weapons, all while learning to navigate the boat under the circumstances of war.

We were a relatively small group of 14 Army MPs, and in a sea of Navy personnel, we stood out, and, hence, had nowhere to hide. Our trainers were all over us, giving us strict lectures about weapon use, engine maintenance and repair, safety and our mission.

The object of our attention was officially called the Patrol Boat River, or PBR. These boats were part of the River Patrol Force and were used to stop and search river traffic in areas such as the Mekong Delta, the Saigon River and in I Corps, in an effort to disrupt weapons shipments. In this role the boats were frequently involved in firefights with enemy soldiers on boats. We were also slated to act as guard boats for barges and supply ships and that seemed to me why Army personnel were being used, since as military police, we were seen as sentries. It was a stretch, but then there was the right way and the Army way. This was the Army way.

The boats were pretty cool, I had to admit. The PBR was a versatile boat with a fiberglass hull and water jet drive which enabled it to operate in shallow, weed-choked rivers. The boat could reach great speed and still be pivoted to reverse direction and, well, turn on a dime. I loved piloting these babies. The River Patrol Boats we trained on were the primary boats in the River Patrol Force. The RPBs were fast and light. They were heavily armed to offset the lack of armor, and were usually equipped with radar, machine guns and grenade launchers. The naval part of the war in Vietnam was not well known, since most of the news sent home was about the air and ground war, not the more intimate and secretive fighting involving small sea craft. The interior boats were part of what was known as the "brown water" Navy. The boat benefited by having heavy firepower—.50 caliber machine guns— because it had so little armor. If we took a hit, the boat might be smashed through and through, so we had to have rapid acceleration and maneuverability to get out of tight situations. Plus, we had to be able to fire back in a flash. In due time, we were out on patrol in the tributaries that snaked about in the area. We would take turns handling the weapons, learning how to dismantle them and fire them (firing ranges away from the boats), and pilot the boat. We would do simulated runs while under fire, and that was damned hairy, for to be fired on from the bushes as we swept down a narrow canal was an adrenaline rush like I'd never experienced. It was too exciting to be scared, but we were scared too, I think.

One night, I was at the wheel when we took a barrage of assimilated fire. I jerked the boat into high gear and took off. The wind was rushing in my face, as I braced to guide the boat down the narrow river, ready to make a sharp 360 degree turn—on a dime— when I met another patrol boat coming directly at me, also going at full speed. We missed each other by a hair. We were all screaming at that point. It was too close for comfort. The bad part was fixing the pumps, figuring the wiring and other mundane but critical stuff to keep the boat in good operating order, if possible, if we were ever hit by enemy fire.

But our time at Mare Island wasn't all work and no play. We were getting a little shaggy hair-wise as the weeks went by. And we were eating like kings at the ample Navy mess hall there. We were always extolling the food and dreading a return to the crappy Army grub we knew we would see again down the road. Our group was more cohesive than the groups I'd been with before. We had to operate as a team and help each other out in close quarters. I was getting to know the guys and having more fun than I'd ever had. Yet, it was still tense since we all knew we were headed for dangerous times abroad. I think we were putting the future out of our minds, in some ways. We had a mixed group: southerners, northerners, California dreamers, dry Midwest types, liberals, conservatives and guys just out for adventure.

We were generally doubtful about Vietnam, but were still enthralled by our own place in the crazy saga, since we were learning to shoot and fly on our magic boats. Being a bit older than most of my buddies, having read about the war to a fault, I knew we were courting trouble by simply going to Nam, and on river patrol boats, were courting double-trouble, all for a dubious cause.

I was very conflicted. I didn't want to say much negative because I wanted the other guys to think they could depend on me. I tended to stay to myself; I didn't want to get caught up in the play atmosphere that was developing. A lot of guys were beginning to want to fight the enemy just so they could fire the guns for real, so they could gun the boats to their maximum, and the where or why of it didn't matter to them.

However, away from the boats, we mostly talked music or social stuff. We often had music blaring in the background while in our barracks. One guy lived off the songs of Crosby, Stills, Nash and Young. This was our favorite group, by far. I was also hearing "Black Magic Woman" by Santana, "Paranoid" by Black Sabbath, and "Who'll Stop the Rain" by Creedence Clearwater Revival. And there was always the Beatles.

There was a good old boy I took a shine to, named Luke, from Texas. He was steady and slow, but the type of man I would want with me if there was trouble. On this particular morning, we were all sitting around the barracks, catching up on our letters, polishing our boots and so on. I had just heard that the former governor of Texas, John Connelly—an old sidekick of Lyndon Johnson—but now a Republican— had been appointed by President Nixon to be secretary of the treasury. Being a political junkie, I thought this was big news and something a guy from Texas might be impressed by, so I made my way over to old Luke, still bent low polishing his boots.

"Hey Luke, heard the news about Governor Connelly," I asked.

Without looking up, he said, "No. Ain't heard nothing."

"Well, Nixon has appointed Governor Connelly the new secretary of the treasury."

"For the whole country?" he asked.

"Yes, he is now the secretary of the treasury for the whole country," I said.

Again, without looking up, he said," Well, old John should be happy. Instead of stealing from one state, he can steal from all fifty."

Old Luke knew his man. Big John Connelly, a protégé of LBJ, was another one of those giant Texas politicians who, somehow, had become filthy rich over the course of his career as a public servant. I walked away, chuckling at Luke's wry sagacity.

4

Although I was learning to relax around my buddies, I still had to overcome my passive-aggressive behavior fueled by my need to protest, yet again, against the military powers that be, and the American involvement in Vietnam. I got the crazy idea that I could deliberately fail the training and be kept stateside. In the beginning, I half-tried in class, while I brought up the rear in the hands-on parts of the training. But it was not my nature to be a laggard. I was embarrassing myself. I had fumbled around at tying knots, piloting the boat, and had haphazardly marked my answers on tests, but I could not live with myself. I had to do a lot of stuff in tandem with the other guys, so I found myself kicking into gear. Lest I not work out the intricacies between cooperating and protesting, I received a harsh reminder of how interdependent we guys were to the whole effort when we went out on a river boat bivouac deep in the tributaries off Mare Island. We were set to run live exercises on the boats, under simulated fire, and would sleep in a Quonset hut located on the water's edge.

I had been delayed reaching the designated site due to an emergency dental procedure I had to have. I had to break off from the group just as we were set to launch our boats from the dock. My tooth was killing me. I caught a ride in a jeep and made a bee-line to the post dental office. I almost ran to the chair. Yet, despite my agony, the Navy dentist scared me right off the bat, when he began griping about being tired from staying up late the night before smoking pot. My anxiety was not quelled, either, by him having the sounds of the musical, "Jesus Christ Superstar," booming throughout the office. All that was missing were beads and incense. But he turned out to be a dentist first, and a disaffected Naval officer second, much to my relief, and I escaped with my ailing tooth duly repaired.

So delayed, I got out to our site by virtue of hitching a ride on a long, slow barge that was heading in the same direction for some reason. I was forced to pilot the behemoth when the regular pilot handed the wheel over to me while he went inside to catch a few winks. He told me to keep the thing in the middle of the broad channel and call for him in an hour. Along the way, I will never forget passing by Suisun Bay where a fleet of battleships from the Second World War were lined up as far as the eye could see. They were like lost ghost ships. I shuddered to think of the stories that could be told from the life and times of those ships, now mothballed in a watery grave.

After a couple of hours, I finally reached shore and joined my team. My first task was to find a guy name Phil, who was supposed to have my sleeping bag. I had arranged with him to pick mine up since I had had to leave the group to go to the dentist before the bags had been distributed. The nights in March were still very cold, especially near the water, so the bags were essential to have. I spotted him standing near the Quonset hut, taking a smoke break.

"Hey, Phil," I said, running up to him. "Where's my sleeping bag?"

"Ah, sleeping bag?"

"Yeah, you were supposed to get mine."

"Well, shit. I forgot. Sorry."

"Forgot! I'll need it tonight. It'll be cold as hell."

"Well, tough titties, Charlie," he said, shrugging his shoulders.

Another draftee, I thought. I glared at him and went off in a huff. The irony that I thought Phil was slack because he was drafted, like me, was not lost on me.

That night, I was the only guy without a sleeping bag. I froze, pure and simple. The chilly, frosty air went right through that corrugated metal, and all I could do was squeeze into a tight knot to keep myself contained. I froze the next night, as well. I learned the hard way that teamwork is critical to one and all, good war or bad war. I got a first-hand lesson on that outing about what being selfish can do to an operation. I knew I didn't want to be the cause of anybody else suffering as I had, due to thinking only of myself.

So, I realized that we had to work together to survive as a hospitable group. My anti-war thinking so deeply implanted in my mind during my college years was too ephemeral to hold up as a counterbalance to my obligation, as I increasingly saw it, to do right by my fellow river boat colleagues in arms.

Another experience that stood out for me during my brief stay in the Frisco area was the time I made my way to the liberal, "Make Love, Not War" and "Free Speech" campus of the University of California, Berkley in Oakland. This was hippie heaven. Alice's Restaurant was nearby, made famous by Arlo Guthrie. On campus, I could see only longhaired, floppy clothed kids, many playing Frisbee, or reading, or strumming a guitar. San Francisco was the west coast haven for hippies, who to me were beatniks with a makeover. My older brother, Ted, had been a beatnik wannabe, what with his poetic ways, tapping on his bongo drums and so forth. But now it was the age of the hippies, who were intriguing to me, along with the psychedelic music that permeated the air at that time, especially in California.

I saw these kids living communally in large, inexpensive Victorian apartments in the Haight-Ashbury section, where I sometimes hung out. The big local bands were also becoming known throughout the country by this time, such as Jefferson Airplane, Big Brother and the Holding Company (Janice Joplin) and the Grateful Dead. Being in San Francisco was thrilling to me, from the standpoint of its counter-culture status, because I remember loving the song by Scott McKenzie entitled simply, "San Francisco" and it became a hit in the United States and Europe. The lyrics inspired thousands of young people from all over the world to travel to San Francisco, sometimes wearing flowers in their hair and distributing flowers to passersby, earning them the name, "Flower Children." I was handed flowers when I was in "the Haight" and was given a Bible, as well, by roving bands of hippie "Jesus Freaks," another youth phenomenon around there for a brief time.

So, when I was actually on the Berkley campus, I thought I was in the very core of this beautiful movement. The girls were barefooted or wearing sandals, had tie-dyed garments, and were braless! And the guys had beards, long hair, and often bell-bottom pants. By their distinctive appearance, hippies were wearing their protest against the conventional world, and distancing themselves from the "straight" and "square" segments of society. I saw hippies through rose-colored glasses. I thought all the best of human behavior—altruism, mysticism, honesty, joy and nonviolence—were, through them, in my midst.

That was until I tried to talk to those hippies.

What I forgot was that I was not a hippie. The hippies saw me as a "straight" intruder, as far as I could tell. "Straight" in those days referred to conventional behavior or appearance, not to sexual orientation. My overtures to the kids I met at Berkley were ignored, or I was treated with a thin veil of politeness. I dressed conventionally—khaki pants and blue dress—because that was all I had to wear. I didn't connect my outer appearance with my inner values, but the Berkley students did. My straight appearance, including my close-cropped hair and Southern accent, was a give-away to a caricature they hated. After a while, I gave up, tired of being brushed off. I stifled my hurt feelings, and found a bus to return to Mare Island.

Screw them, I thought. *You all wear a uniform as much as I do. Wall Street suits, Berkley suits, what's the difference, if you have to have a damn suit.*

After eight weeks of training, I completed the course and received my certificate to pilot the river patrol boats, despite my problems with night vision (glare of lights blinded me with my extreme near-sightedness and thick glasses), along with my slowness to repair the motor parts. Yet, I was able to do it all well enough to get by.

I continued to travel to San Francisco on the

weekends, but I was less enamored with the "Flower Children." I found comfort in sitting around old neighborhood Irish bars where I could talk to real people without loud music drowning us out, seeing Wilt Chamberlain play at the Cow Palace, touring about the exotic Chinese section of the city, and seeing with amazement the tawdry stretch of strip clubs, bars and porno shops on Market Street. I also marveled at rows of Hare Krishna's, all men—shaved heads except for a pigtail in back, in long robes and sandals, chanting and singing in a spiritual state of peace. I didn't know what to make of them. I did like their aura of love. I never felt such an aura from the old time religion preachers I'd heard in the past.

At long last, I reported to the Oakland Army reception station to report for duty and deployment to South Vietnam. I did show up, after all, even though we had three extra days to frolic in San Francisco. By that time, our little band of river boat rats had become close. We were a team that knew its tasks, if not its mission. And that was my problem.

Back to the situation at hand at Long Binh following the captain's dramatic news we could go river boat or not, our band of river boat boys began to argue about whether to stay with it, or transfer. Some of us wanted to stay on the boats, others wanted out. But most of the guys wanted to get out on the rivers and see what the boats could do. Many of them were acting gung-ho at this moment. The momentum was building for us to stay as one and hit the water.

My heart was pulling me to them; my head was holding me back. *Why go? For what purpose?* I thought. I had not had many choices up to this point. I'd had to go where I was told to go, do what I was told to do. This time, it was up to me. If I went with the flow, I'd go riverboat, but if I went my own way, I'd stay inland. I decided I wanted to transfer back to a military police posting. When I made my feelings known, the crew converged on me, pleading with me to stay.

"What do you mean, Charlie? Let's stay together, man. Kick ass, together," one guy yelled at me, flush with excitement.

"Naw, sorry, but I want to go MP," I said, now feeling really shitty about my decision, but determined to not be swayed. I liked my comrades, but I felt the river boat duty was not wise, especially since the Vietnamese would be taking it over in a month or two. I had heard through the grapevine in the two days we'd been in 'Nam that we were carrying out few, if any, offensive initiatives. Frankly, I didn't feel it was justified to go on the last remaining hazardous duty when there was no clear military objective, anymore.

"Ah, come on, man, stay with us. We've gone this far, let's stick it out," another friend said. I remained adamant that I was going on my own. After a few minutes more of trying to persuade me, the guys sort of shrugged and moved on to the river boat area to get their personnel packages and get situated for their assignment. I believe one more guy opted out, but I really can't remember.

Although I was resolved in my mind that separating was the right thing to do, in my heart, I felt like I was letting my friends down. It was all I could do to restrain myself from changing my mind and running after my buddies, no matter how dumb it might seem to me. But I remained still, even as I wiped away a tear, and watched them until they disappeared on the way to the river area. I walked over to the general assignment area by myself. I had never felt so guilty in my life. Nobody had accused me of being unafraid, but I felt they were thinking it. Yet, rarely did many soldiers, at this stage, take crazy chances. We all knew we were in a bad place, so we never put pressure on anybody to be a hero. And my boat buddies knew what they were doing and, given a choice, didn't expect me to go with them if I didn't want to go.

Thankfully, within two months every single member of our River Boat Patrol was transferred to Saigon, all safe and sound. I heard their time on the rivers was boring, but given the alternative, they weren't complaining too much. The mixture of boredom and terror is a stable of warfare. Most of time nothing happens, but when it does, the fireworks can come at any moment. To know they all made it back safely was the best news I could hope to hear. Yet, I wondered again if I should have gone with them. We sometimes suffer forever for our decisions, even if they are the right ones.

As luck would have it, I got assigned to Saigon. It didn't have to happen that way, either. I was standing in a small group of soldiers waiting on a very bored corporal to hand out assignments to us. He was picking up personnel files that were stacked on a table next to him. He was picking randomly from this stack of files to send us to areas that ranged from safe to very dangerous. I knew about where my personnel file was located, which was just behind him. However, he was calling out names from the file next to him. I could see he was not likely to go to my file, unless he was prompted to do so. When he said that the next five names would be going to Saigon, my ears perked up.

"Listen up, people. These next five are for Saigon," the corporal said. "If you have kin there, or a friend, let me know."

Then he began to select the names, but still from the file next to him, not from the files behind him, where my file was located. I saw right then and there that my fate was in his hands, or it was in my hands. I had to intervene immediately, or my fate would be decided by mere happenstance. *I've got to do something, now!* I thought.

I pushed ahead and called out to the corporal.

"Hey, corporal, I know a guy in Saigon. We were in MP school together."

This was, in fact, true, because I had recently gotten a letter from this guy, Jim, who had told me he was stationed in Saigon. Jim had gone straight from Fort Gordon to Vietnam, evidently. I was behind him by a few months, due to being at Mare Island. The corporal stopped and asked my name. I told him and then let him know my file was directly behind him, not in the pile he was picking from to his right. He nodded his head, turned and picked up the small stack behind him, flipped through it, pulled out my file, and then called out my name. I walked forward and he leaned down from his platform and gave me my file, now stamped "destination Saigon." The exchange took seconds and the corporal gave it no thought. I had been lucky and made my own luck at the same time.

I looked around and all the other soldiers were simply standing there, almost like sheep, just waiting to see where they would be sent. Again, I had pangs of guilt over my manipulation of the process. But I still felt I was working within the system, had not lied, and had simply seen opportunity staring at me. Opportunity knocked, in my view, and I opened the door. I wasn't sure if I was in good shape or not with my assignment; although I figured I'd drawn a good pick. I also knew that Vietnam had no front lines or rear guards in a pure sense. The enemy was everywhere; we could not tell friend from foe, so no matter where I was assigned, I was still going to have to be on my toes, even in Saigon.

As I settled in for my last night at Long Binh, I still couldn't believe I was actually in this benighted country, at long last. I remembered watching Walter Cronkite describing the Vietnam conflict on the nightly news, usually giving us a body count, as if it was a gruesome athletic contest that was to be decided by who had the most kills and injuries at the end of it. I would take note of it, gather up my books and go to the library to study, or hang out, never thinking I'd be in the spot I was in now, almost five years from those fateful telecasts.

I knew this "miserable war," as I had called it back home, was beginning to draw down, but I couldn't tell it from what I was seeing around me. The Long Binh Army Post appeared to be the equal of a fairly good-sized town. It was crowded with Americans and Vietnamese working at their tasks, almost in a carefree manner. The post had dental clinics, large restaurants, and snack bars. There was a Post Exchange, a huge swimming pool, basketball and tennis courts, a golf driving range, University of Maryland extension classes, a bowling alley, many nightclubs with live music, a Chase Manhattan Bank branch, a branch laundry services and a massage parlor. Long Binh also included the Long Binh Stockade, or jail, which was nicknamed LBJ for "Long Binh Jail."

My God, if we declared we were leaving tomorrow, it would take six-months to load this stuff out of here. We ain't going anywhere, anytime soon, I figured. *There is too much money invested here to leave quickly, no matter how much blood flows.*

The next day our little group of military police designees met for the ride to Saigon, about twenty miles south. We loaded our duffle bags onto the rear of a military cargo truck, popularly known as a deuce-and-a-half, and climbed on. The road was paved, but had its fair share of potholes, so the ride was bumpy and with the tropical weather in full force, very hot. One of the guys was a real hothead ready to kill every Vietnamese he saw. I was glad we hadn't been issued any weapons yet, for this fool looked ready to shoot on sight any Asian he encountered. He was a Kansan named Larry.

"Hey, Larry, you need to chill, if you gonna make it a whole year," said Staff Sergeant Mack Shepherd, the oldest guy on board, and the ranking member of our group.

"Well, we got to win this thing, beat these commie assholes to hell, where they belong," Larry said, eyes wide now with resentment.

I couldn't help myself. "Larry, I heard the French lost this war about twenty years ago. What did they want with this hell-hole, anyway?" I asked.

"Hell if I know," Larry said, not happy to be questioned, preferring to have us just listen.

"What if this fight is just for France to keep this place, so they can run it, like they used to do?"

"Fuck that. I want to kill commies."

"Actually, Larry, America and France were allies in World War II. You know, friends. After we saved France's ass from the Nazis, we helped them to try and hold on to this place. Old Ho Chi Minh and his commie pals fought to keep them out."

"No shit, old Ho, Ho, Ho was fighting us that far back?"

"Yeah, when Harry Truman took over, he let a pile of money go to keeping France's head above water. I think all the big-wig Vietnamese and old royalty were on our side. They were mostly Catholic. The French converted the elites here long ago," I said, enjoying being a teacher.

"Catholics? These gooks don't have no religion, except Buddha, or some voodoo shit like that," Larry snorted.

To my surprise, Staff Sergeant Shepherd leaned in and gave me a little help.

"You're right about Catholics being here," he said, as he cupped his hands over his cigarette to light it.

He had been around, I could tell. I appreciated him speaking up. I thought lifers like him were generally ignorant of the history of Vietnam. Guys like him stayed in the military because they couldn't hack it in the outside world. Case closed. But this fellow, I was learning, could hold his own.

"Yeah, and the French fought hard here," he continued. "It was French blood and American money, all right."

"Why did France want this goddam place?" Larry asked, now becoming curious about the backstory for this beleaguered country we had come to save.

"Well, Larry, France is a pretty powerful country and throughout the years has gone out and taken over little countries, more than just Vietnam, really, parts of Africa and other Asian regions, usually to get their raw materials, or some advantage. The whole rotten practice is called colonialism." I said.

"America frees people, Jack, so I don't buy us helping a country take over a country just to make money," Larry said, folding his arms in defiance. I like his answer, warming up to Jack's patriotic instincts.

"Ha, now you're catching on, Larry. Well, France gave up after getting whipped in a big battle called, let's see, yes, Dienbienphu, in 1954, and then we picked up the baton. Kind of on the sly while Eisenhower and Kennedy were in office, but full swing with ground troops under LBJ," I explained.

Larry was staring at me with a blank look on his face. I couldn't tell if I was getting through or not.

"Yep, Larry, we've had American grunts here since 1965. Six frickin' years, my friend," I said, leaning back on the truck rail.

Another newbie chimed in. Billy was his name, a Florida kid. "Hey, I know these gooks are all commies. I say, if we don't get 'em here, their crap spreads everywhere. Scary shit, man."

"True, Billy," said Staff Sergeant Shepherd, "old Ho Chi Minh is the head honcho for the Communists, been in the jungles for a long time. The peasants all over, north and south, love him. Those bastards don't mind dying, either, and they don't mind waiting. That's what scares me. I reckon they are Communist by name, but what makes them fight ain't no Communist theory, they just hate foreigners messing with their country, especially the Chinese. They want to run this country on their own."

"You know it, Staff Sergeant," I said. "I've read that Ho Chi Minh would fight either communist China or the Soviet Union if they tried to take over Vietnam, just as quick as he's fighting us."

"Yeah," Staff Sergeant Shepherd said. "Let me tell you, boys, Ho hates the Chinese most of all. I read somewhere that Ho told his people to fear the Chinese the most because they are over here. China is not here today and gone tomorrow. China borders this shitty little country and hangs over them like a low, dark cloud. But old Ho knows France and America are foreigners; he knows we'll leave eventually. Ho said 'I'd rather smell French shit for five years than eat Chinese shit for the rest of my life.'" We laughed, while the message hit home loud and clear.

So, we continued to talk it all out as we got closer to Saigon, even as we began to see more guards and barbed wire fences and sandbags amid the defensive parameters.

We all tired of talking about Vietnamese political history as we got closer to the allures of Saigon, three million strong, full of bars, bordellos and other amusements for American G.I.s. We also had been warned, on the other hand, that there were about five thousand Viet Cong in the city boundaries, which were also ready to give us their own version of a welcome. The Cong were southern Vietnamese fighting for the communist side. They were infiltrators, in the guerrilla-fighting mode, more than being a regular army like the huge North Vietnamese Army. But they could kill you, all the same, if you got in their way, even in the middle of Saigon.

Billy's fear that a communist win in Vietnam would allow the philosophy to spread was not just his own narrow minded thinking. Many political leaders and scholars of the day believed the same thing. American leaders, in particular, feared that helping the independent efforts in Vietnam in those days was going to contribute to the larger danger to world stability: spreading, monolithic communism, aka, the "Red Menace." Nevertheless, I had my doubts it was that simple. I was lost in my thoughts about the big picture, but I was getting edgy about the emerging capitol city of South Vietnam. But I had one more question for the impressive SSG Shepherd.

"Staff Sergeant, I have to know, why have you returned to this place? You seem to doubt our official rationale for being here? Why not speak out to the brass about this mess?" I said, leaning in with great intensity.

"Son, I know you're smart. We've learned some stuff from you, but you don't know it all. First thing, I'm a lifer, so you're probably surprised I know a damn thing besides doing what I'm told to do."

I was embarrassed that he had read me so well. I was learning by painful experience that I had been selling professional soldiers short on their intelligence.

"What's more, I choose to be here, as most lifers do, unlike you draftees. That old adage you mock, 'Ours is not to reason why, ours is to do or die,' is not as stupid as you think. Every country needs somebody to fight its battles. The leaders can't lead if its army and navy and such can balk at every order given, or at every assignment given, and so on. I love my country and I follow orders, even if I know the orders are dumb as dirt. I don't mean the off the wall orders that are crazy wrong, but about everything else. Somebody has to do it," he said, as he settled back against his seat, looking a little exasperated at me for questioning what was at the heart of his profession: allegiance to the military code of conduct in peace or at war.

"I'm sorry, Staff Sergeant. I know you don't set policy. I know better than that, but I forget it, sometimes. We guys in uniform can't do anything we please, not even the brass. I see where you're coming from, I guess." I reluctantly saw his point. I felt a little ashamed for having been so snooty about lifers. I'd been pushing a fine line between talking bad about foreign policy, which was not set by the military, and the military itself, which the sergeant was a proud member of.

"That's right, soldier. And don't forget, we are forbidden by law to speak out publicly against this war. We don't gripe out loud against any military action we have to take. Our freedom of expression is not like a civilian's, and that's okay. We have to be real careful about talking back to officers or non-commission officers, too. So, that's that. But, you better damn believe that I'll be writing letters to the editor when I retire," he said, chuckling.

For the first time, I could see that this misguided war was not just a tragedy for the people, it was a double tragedy for the many conscientious soldiers that were obliged by their military oath to administer the battle, to bear its stresses and its brutality, and to do so regardless of their own opinions about what they had to do.

Seeing soldiers, like Staff Sergeant Shepherd, doing their job, even when they had doubts about the policy behind it, and putting country over their own interests, was making a deep impression on me. For the first time in my life, I was beginning to see the selflessness by our troops as a form of high patriotism on a par, if not higher, than the patriotism I had been applying disproportionately, up to this point, to anti-war protestors.

5

By the time we entered the outskirts of Saigon, we had exhausted ourselves by our intense conversation about the why and how of being in Vietnam. We had enjoyed having our say, but it was now time to be alert and watch each other's back. The crowds were growing now as we went through a check point, waved along by serious looking guards. We became engulfed in a sea of humanity of a like I'd never seen in my life.

I saw people of all colors, shapes and nationalities. Although they were mostly Southeastern Asians, I wasn't sure they were all Vietnamese. I couldn't tell a Vietnamese from a Cambodian or a Chinese, but I had been told I'd better figure it out fast, or I'd get my tail whipped by the Asian I misidentified, if I did it to his face. Whew! And I thought it was bad back home in the South. The noise was panoramic, part human and part traffic, but all of it at full force. The chattering in Vietnamese or other similar dialects was like an out-of-tune piano being played hard and fast, and all incomprehensible to me.

And the conveyances on the road were mind-boggling: vans, old big automobiles, dusty old taxis, trucks of all sizes—many belching out kerosene in black plums through their tail pipes—bicycles, Pedi-cabs (motorized rickshaws), rickshaws (man-pedaled) and, mainly, motorcycles. The traffic was crazy: no rules, no stop lights, and at intersections the right-of-way went to who was there first with the biggest vehicle. The fleet of taxis was old Peugeot models painted blue and yellow that had been left to the Vietnamese by the French. They all had to be at least eighteen years old.

I also saw animals in and out of the traffic, anything from dogs to chickens to cows. Saigon was a busy place, and I could see beauty in many of its buildings, mostly French in influence. There were once parks, restaurants and hotels so in abundance that Saigon was known as the "Paris of the Orient." But the city had become downtrodden. The once picturesque city had become infested with squatter's shacks and other pervasive signs of poverty. I saw homeless looking people bathing their children in the stagnant water in the gutters, some sleeping in doorways or on park benches.

But the commotion was thrilling, in a way, because it was so exotic to me. My sense of danger began to fade the more we drove through the crowds. It was probably a false sense of security, but I had no way of telling friend from foe. We were helpless if we had come under attack, since we had not been issued any weapons yet. I got caught up in the buzz of the crowd and began smiling at the hordes of people, some of them waving at me, yelling or begging for money. Women squatted in the road behind open baskets of rice, fruits, and metal trays piled with fish, many infested with flies. Since we were on the move in the back of the lumbering deuce-and-a-half, we were up higher than street level, so we felt things were safe enough. Although excited, we didn't want our luck to run out, so we were anxious to get to our destination, where we wouldn't be on such public display. Eventually, we reached our post unscathed.

My nostrils were taking a hit, as well: rancid aromas from the high piles of trash gathered on the roadsides were brutal. Then the corner fish markets matched the uncollected trash with their produce soaked in a god-awful Vietnam concoction of fermented fish oil sauce called nuoc mam, as putrid a smell as I ever had to inhale. The fish markets would be with us for the whole one-year tour, but we soon adjusted to all the strange new smells of the market place, not all of them bad, by the way. I learned that the Vietnamese thought we were pretty smelly, too.

Different diets, I suppose.

Although I developed an affinity for the local merchants on the street, I was always afraid to taste any food straight from the market stalls. And the military brass actually forbade American soldiers from drinking local water, since the water came straight from the Saigon River and was heavily contaminated. For the soldiers who foolishly drank local water anyway, one bout with a waterborne disease such as Hepatitis A, or abdominal cramps or watery diarrhea was enough to keep them on the straight and narrow from there on end. Thankfully, we were able to get safe water from our own U. S. controlled water treatment facilities.

At last, we arrived in an American fortified area still inside the city limits of Saigon. We got off the truck and gathered in an open area next to a series of tented structures protected from the heat by netting on the sides. I found a spot and after a little chit-chat, I could see the hardened faces around me as a far cry from the innocent kids we all were on our first day in the Army.

When the big day arrived, I had to report to the Raleigh based Army Induction Center. My mother took me to Lillington, a nearby town, to catch a bus for the 30-mile trip. She and I sipped coffee at a café, just making casual talk until the bus arrived on its route from Fayetteville, home to Fort Bragg, a major Army post. I figured I might wind up in Fayetteville before long, but who was to know at this point? The bus arrived and came to a stop in front of the café. I gave Mother a long hug outside. She was teary eyed and held me as long as she could. I also waved good-bye to the café owner, Jimmy the Greek, as he was called, who had followed us outside, and seemed to want a hug too. I stepped across the gravel parking lot and climbed on the bus to begin my journey.

I felt cut off from my natural world right away, for although I'd taken this route many times before to Raleigh, it had always been in the comfort of a car, not on a form of public transportation. I was already sniffing my nose at this first small indignity upon my exalted civilian status. And, oh, I was dreaming of how nice it would be to be back at Mr. Henry's in Washington, drinking beer and talking politics, or girls, or music with friends. But I knew those days were in my past, not in my near future.

I got to the station located on St. Mary's Street across from Rex Hospital, where I was born. It was familiar territory, but I couldn't lounge around and reminisce. I found myself in a room with other draftees, and it was a mix of white, brown and black guys, and some I wasn't sure about. The chatter was light, some making funny remarks, and some silent, lost in their last thoughts as civilians. I was doing all right but the whole scene was alien to anything I'd ever seen. Soon enough, we were shuffled into a medical room, the size of an average living room, where we were told to form a circle. Then the Army doctor came in and began to give us orders.

"All right, boys, drop your socks and show me your cocks," he said, chuckling slightly. *What*? I thought. We were not smiling. We then had to turn our backs to him and face the wall, dropping our pants so he could check our privates. This was downright humiliating, no matter if the doctor found humor in it. I never lied on any of the forms, but if I had written down I had taken illegal drugs, had explored *"homosexual relations,"* or had seen a psychiatrist, I would have been given a much closer look before I was accepted. Declaring oneself a "conscientious objector" was a popular diversionary tactic then, too.

I just told the truth on the questions and waited like a lamb for the next set of directives. The part that really cheered me up was filling out a life insurance form. The young lady taking the information casually asked me, "Who would be your beneficiary in case you are killed?" *Whoa, crap, don't say that*? I thought. But I answered it, naming my mother. This part made the whole experience go from being surreal to, well, real. My spirits were sinking.

After a while, we had been poked, prodded, lined up, advised and, at last, lined up in a tiny room to take our oath. The Army officer stood before us and had us raise our right hand. I took note of the American flag and other official symbols, and it gave the assembly a sense of dignity, even if we were there by coercion, not invitation. I couldn't help myself from trying my best to stand erect and give a snappy salute to the officer after the ceremonies had been completed.

The enlisted oath we recited went like this:

"I, Charles Malone, do solemnly swear that I will support and defend the Constitution of the United States against all enemies, foreign and domestic; that I will bear true faith and allegiance to the same; and that I will obey the orders of the President of the United States and the orders of the officers appointed over me, according to regulations and the Uniform Code of Military Justice. So help me God."

At that moment, the atmosphere took a chilly change. The wry smile on the face of our keeper, a sergeant, told me we were no longer guests, but his wards. He stepped forward to bark out some new orders, not asking us anymore, but telling us flat out what to do. We were given directives to stay the night at the local Sir Walter Raleigh Hotel and be back the next day, bright and early, for assignment to an Army post, somewhere. I thought, *Crap, I'm in it now.*

The next morning we gathered in the Sir Walter dining room, where we were forced to eat in a corner of the restaurant, away from the civilians, who were casually going about unhindered. I felt angry at this isolation. I was used to doing as I pleased in a hotel, not to be herded into a corner. My civilian past was clearly at war with my Army reality. I was almost relieved when we scrambled into the van to take us to the induction center for our final processing.

By that afternoon I was being taken by van for a plane ride to Louisiana, destination Fort Polk, a.k.a, "Tiger Land." *Good God!* I thought. The van ride from the processing center on St. Mary's Street in Raleigh to the Raleigh-Durham Airport, in my mind, was like walking down death row to face my execution.

There were about seven of us going to Fort Polk. We were nervous, chattering away. It had been assumed we would be heading for nearby Fort Bragg, about 60 miles south of Raleigh. But we were surprised to making the long flight to parts unknown. I was quickly finding out that the Army way was usually not the economical way. Why not send us to Fayetteville? It would be much cheaper, but what did I know?

We landed in New Orleans. Although we were dazzled by the luminous lights flickering up to us in the air, once on ground, we were hurriedly sent into a waiting area within the sprawling confines of the airport. Our holding area was a typical airport interior, all sleek with lots of glass and chrome. The chairs were vinyl and in rows. We shuffled around, but dared not leave the area since we were set to transfer to a smaller plane. After about an hour we were led to a commuter plane, which held about 15 passengers. We scampered into it, fastened our seatbelts and took off again, this time heading to the west-central part of Louisiana. It was dark inside and out, except for the bright red lights coming off the instrument panel in the cockpit. We were quiet now, transfixed on our ensuing adventure to strange new destinations.

At last, we landed just outside of Fort Polk. We got off and were guided to a small cinderblock building. We were on an isolated spot on post. We could see vast areas of open fields and chain link fences beyond the gray cement runway. It felt like a clandestine meet up from a spy novel. We didn't tarry, as it was late at night, around 2 o'clock in the morning. We took a small van to for a short ride to a mess hall, surprisingly, still open. A lone mess cook prepared hamburgers for us. It wasn't bad, I had to admit, yet I was so hungry, even Army food tasted good. *So far, so good*, I thought.

At long last, we were sent to a mostly empty barrack. It was an old white wooden facility, and I got into the bottom section of a two-tier bunk. Settling in and stretching out on the bed, I could see the moon outside, shrouded by moving clouds. But sleep wouldn't come easily. All around me was stillness. The inside of the barrack had a peculiar smell to it, kind of like the sweaty smell of a locker room. The bathroom reeked of Pine-Sol. All in all, it was not unpleasant, just alien to what I was used to. I could hear somebody faintly snoring from another location, and I could hear chatter outside from time to time. I lay there, just in wonder that I was in this barrack, in this place and in this situation. My head was both full of doubt and anticipation. I then tried to get some sleep because we were under orders to be up at the ungodly hour of 6:00 a.m. to meet in formation.

My strategy was to survive this ordeal, and that meant staying out of trouble. I was too much the 90-pound weakling to out-muscle anyone, so I thought staying invisible would be a good policy for self-preservation. At this embryonic stage of my military career, I was taking on the persona of a prisoner-of-war more than that of a soldier.

Fort Polk was situated in a pine forest with heavy underbrush, which duplicated somewhat the terrain and conditions to be found in Vietnam. It was located about 250 miles north of New Orleans. In the early 1960s, Fort Polk began converting to an infantry training center. A small portion of the fort was filled with dense, jungle-like vegetation, and this helped commanders prepare their units for battle in Southeast Asia. This training area became known as Tiger Land. We would learn to dread the thought that, upon graduation from basic training, we might be assigned to advance infantry training, for that meant an automatic ticket to Vietnam: as a "grunt." More soldiers were shipped to Vietnam from Fort Polk than from any other base, our drill sergeants often reminded us, letting us know that the hell we were in was only a warm up for the hell to come. But before basic, we had to go through processing, which involved about three or four days of indoctrination (getting yelled at), getting new Army clothes, supplies, haircuts, medical exams and setting up our personnel records.

The new world began for me during our first formation. I instinctively found a spot in the middle of the group, wanting to be as unobtrusive as a floating cork in a stream. The drill sergeant stood there silently looking us over. He stood there in an erect way, hands behind his back, uniform starched and boots shiny. He had a wry smile, and his eyes were dancing in anticipation. If he had had a tail, it would have been turning in a slow circle, like a cat ready to pounce on unsuspecting mice. I had a good idea that the nightmare was about ready to commence. We were a slovenly looking group, even I had to admit.

"Attention, men!" We tried to pull ourselves together, but we weren't sure how.

"Oh. My. God. What do we have here!" he said. "I thought I would be assigned men, not a group of women." He began to pace back and forth. "No, no, no. But let me not insult the ladies. I am not going to call you ladies. I will call you a bunch of maggots!" he said. "Where did you all come from? What rock did you all crawl out from under?" He had his hands on his hips, feet firmly planted on the ground, staring at us as if we were exhibits in a zoo.

Well, we love you, too, I thought, almost smirking. But I stayed still.

The drill sergeant was African-American, which I took note of, for I'd never heard a black man yell at white people. It was strange, but quickly I put that out of my mind. I was beginning to rapidly take my measure of a man in the Army, not by the color of his skin, but by the rank on his shoulder. This aspect of the new world threw me off, because theoretically, this was an improvement over the social order I so adored as a civilian. The newbie in front me, a black guy from up north, from the look of him—all jazzed up with an Afro, comb in his hair, wrist bands and an ear ring—was shifting about, already impatient with this old black man preaching at him. His deft movements caught the drill sergeant's eye. He ambled over to the black guy, gave him a hard look, and leaned into him within an inch.

"Well, what do we have here? Mr. Black Panther? You Huey Newton (founder of Black Panthers) himself? I don't think so. Where you from, boy?" he asked in biting words.

"I'm from New Jersey, sir!"

"Sir!" The drill sergeant repeated. Angry now, he leaned in again and screamed at this prey. "I am an enlisted man, Jersey boy, a sergeant, and I work for a living. Only officers are called sir, never call me sir! Repeat, never call me sir!" he said, looking around at all of us. "And that goes for all you maggots. Address me as drill sergeant. I work for a living." He leaned in again, "You got that, Jersey boy?"

"Yes, ah, yes, drill sergeant."

"And what's this shit you wearing?"

"Just cool stuff, drill sergeant," Jersey boy said, revealing a slight grin. "Black power, baby."

This gesture of independence and foolish attempt to bond with the old, black Army lifer was the worst thing this guy could have done. The drill sergeant was hot now. He began to jump around, huffing and cursing at the new recruit.

"Black power? Is this why you wearing this bracelet?" The bracelet was leather, woven thing, just like his necklace. The drill sergeant yanked both of them off, quick as a cat.

"You don't wear this black power shit in this man's Army. You will soon enough lose that Afro, too, you dig, Jersey boy?" The recruit from Jersey was now reduced to a trembling, silent shell of his former cocky self. He was keeping his mouth shut now.

The drill sergeant returned to front and center.

"Listen up, ladies. You have seen Malcolm X over here get his makeover. Any you white boys think you're something special? Maybe you dumbasses think you're Elvis, or a Beatle. Well, step up, dammit, and I'll strip you down, too."

"You are all in the United States Army. You are not at home with your mama. I am your mama now. I am your daddy now. You will be in an Army uniform soon. But, I'll be damned if I'll call you soldiers, yet," he said, pausing to let us reflect on our lowly status. "I will call you dickheads now," he said.

Lowering his voice, he continued. "But you will learn to be soldiers, although it will take a miracle from the looks of you." He lowered his voice, once again, almost to a whisper, to say, "This is day one for you people. Listen to me and you'll make it. If you do not, you do it at your own peril. Listen to me, I say, because your life may depend upon it one day."

His last words sent a chill up me. He may be a brute, I thought, but he makes sense. I hadn't expected to find soldiers talking good sense, to be intelligent. I was confused. My preconceptions about the military were taking a beating, and I didn't like it. But the drill sergeant was not done, and he began yelling again, breaking my revelry.

"Now, get to the mess hall for breakfast! Then get your asses over to that next building with the fucking barber pole, for you are going to get a haircut. Yeah, you black power boys, enjoy your Afro while it lasts; same for you piss-ant hippies. Your golden locks will be gone soon, too. Try not to step on your weenie getting out of my sight. Dismissed!"

We all broke away, like bewildered sheep, rushing to get to the mess hall and away from our new mamma and daddy and God, all wrapped up in one.

Over the next three days we went through the hoops to get our uniforms, which consisted of green fatigues, kaki outfits and dress uniforms. The gear was stuffed in huge canvas duffle bags, so heavy it was hard to lift the weight off the ground. I had to drag my duffle bag to the barrack, since I could not lift it on my shoulders the whole way. I envied the strong, country boys that could easily lift the same load without much effort. The drill sergeants added to the humiliation by belittling us for being weak, but, ironically, their harsh words goaded us to complete that first hard road we had to travel. We eventually got settled into our barracks.

On the eve of our being shipped out for the actual basic training experience, I was in line in an office when a base sergeant, not a drill sergeant, approached me and another recruit, who'd become a friend, just after we had just finished taking a military intelligence test, or something like that.

"Hey, you guys did well on the brain test."

"Thanks, sergeant," I said, wondering why he was making halfway friendly talk.

"Look we need a few guys to help us here in the processing station, to grade tests and so on. I see you guys have some college, so how about staying here for a while? You can go to basic later on."

Let me analyze this situation, I thought. *I can take basic training now in July, or I can take it in the fall. By delaying things a bit, I will avoid roasting to death. This is a no brainer.*

"I accept, sergeant," I said. And within the hour I was taken out of the line of miscreants going to basic on that "Lose E Ana" hot day, given a temporary rank of sergeant, moved out of the bay area, where I was with about thirty guys, and given my own room in a barrack. Jeez, I was doing all right and I had been in the Army for less than a week. It seemed privileges kept coming to me, whether I tried for them or not.

So, for the next six weeks I worked for Sergeant Razzi, who headed up the testing section of the Welcoming Center. It was easy work and we had it made, to be honest.

I even found time to hitch hike one weekend to New Orleans for a fun time in the French Quarter and Bourbon Street. Thumbing across Louisiana was something else. I saw my share of peeling clapboard houses, palm and oak trees, seedy truck stops and low rent bars. I passed by the girders of the Earl K. Long Bridge near Baton Rouge, and smelled the smoke rising from the oil refineries nearby. I knew I was in Cajun country for sure when I passed by a stand of cypress trees, heavy with hanging moss, rooted on the banks of a swamp topped with lily pads and cattails.

The French Quarter, with its quaint buildings, blues music wailing out to the streets, intricate ironworks, courtyards and neon lights, gave the place both a sophisticated and disreputable air. The rich French, Spanish influences were everywhere, along with other international touches. I loved sitting in Preservation Hall on a plain wooden bench listening to some old black guys play jazz, mingling in the crowded bars with the friendliest people I'd ever seen. And I was drawn to the faddish shops that were selling leather belts and bracelets, incense, psychedelic posters, party novelties and rock albums. When I'd walk down the crowded sidewalks, everybody was in a Mardi gras spirit, with both laughter and music always permeating the air. I wanted to stay forever.

I slept in a hostel for one dollar a night, waking up the next morning on a balcony overlooking a side street. There were other sleeping kids all around me. I immediately felt for my back wallet: it was still there. I wondered back to the bathroom, but there was a hippy looking girl vomiting into the toilet, while across the room there were some other kids passed out on a couch. The whole area stank. Except for a single naked light bulb hanging from the ceiling, the hallway was dark. I wanted to say I was being Bohemian, but I felt that was too dignified a label to put on the crummy feeling I had being in the middle of this dilapidated place. I was more than ready to scamper down the rickety steps and get out into the sunshine.

Soon enough, due to having only a weekend pass, I was headed back to camp. I ditched my civilian clothes to hitchhike back. To get a ride, one had to wear a uniform. It meant getting a ride right away. I had a family give me a lift. It was dad and mom in the front seat, me and their daughter in the back. They were proud to help me. I had never gotten this treatment before, certainly not out of uniform. It registered with me that my jaded view of the military was not shared by Middle America. So, as the weeks rolled by since I had arrived at Fort Polk, I had still not soiled my uniform or been ordered to do anything put push a pencil. I had not marched, held a weapon or done any physical exercise. I even had the experience of seeing the jazz legend Duke Ellington and his orchestra perform on post, front row, too. But my time in paradise would not last forever.

One day we were in the administrative center shifting through the test results when a visiting general came through. We had gotten notice he would be by to inspect our procedures. We felt ready for him. Sergeant Razzi was standing by, gently rocking back and forth on his heels, knowing his college boys would do a good job explaining the testing and grading process. The general was duly impressed with it all, noted our good works—part of which I explained to him—and seemed set to leave, when he stopped and asked us a few questions. This was when the trouble began.

"Good work, private. I like the way you explained the process," the general said amiably.

"Thank you, sir." I wondered if this old fellow had even understood the process I had explained. My civilian prejudices still flowed; I still felt "military intelligence" was an oxymoron.

"Yes, well, private, carry on. Good job, everybody." Then he paused, and, as an afterthought, asked one more question. "Ah, by the way, son, where did you take basic training?"

Oh, holy crap, I thought, trying not to panic.

"Ah, to be honest sir, we haven't taken basic training yet," I said, glancing at Sergeant Razzi, who was now putting his hand to his face.

"What? You haven't taken basic? How long you been in the Army, son?" the general asked, his face now a portrait of suspicion.

"Ah, sir, we've been in the Army about six weeks."

"Six weeks?" the general exclaimed. He shifted his gaze to Sergeant Razzi and the local officer, giving them both a hard look.

"What's going on here? I see these fellows are doing a good job, but did you think they could do your work forever? These young men are in the Army to learn to be soldiers first, not clerks," he said. He looked directly at our sergeant and the captain there and said, "Get your priorities in order, and I mean right away!"

The captain overseeing our administrative unit stepped forward, also staring hard at Sergeant Razzi, and assured the general that the situation would be corrected forthwith. Once the general was gone, the captain proceeded to chew out Sergeant Razzi. I stood there helplessly, knowing the curtains on our little masquerade were quickly coming down.

6

How could I ever have thought my extended time as a temporary sergeant in the Fort Polk reception center would go on without notice from the higher ups? I thought, as I continued to wait for assignment sitting cross legged in the dusty field somewhere in the bowls of Saigon. It was terribly hot. I took a swig of water from my canteen. I noticed the traffic nearby, its fury never ending, it seemed. I could not imagine driving in it. But I knew I probably would before too long. The density of the city was almost overwhelming; the urban din was relentless. I leaned back at let my mind wondered back to what happened to me after my long tenure in the reception center was exposed. I got a rude awakening, to say the least.

Three days later I was in line with about 30 other fresh recruits marching double time down a dirt path to the basic training compound across the road from the well-manicured lawns surrounding the induction center I'd been housed in for my first six-weeks in the Army. As such, I was experiencing my first day in the real Army. As I hustled to keep up, reality was hitting me hard: my temporary rank gone, my private room gone, and my sense of privilege gone. I was just one more lowly private now. The insignia now gone, other privates would no longer be deferred to me due to the sergeant patch that had adorned my shoulder. I would be the one jumping to orders now, not the other way around. Yet, I was able to take some satisfaction that I was going through all that stress in the mild weather of autumn, instead of the hell of summer.

Around 5 o'clock in the morning, I was rousted out of my sleep by the shrill sound of an iron pipe being banged inside a metal trashcan by the drill sergeant. The ear-splitting sound from the trash can, the screaming from the drill sergeant to get the hell up, along with our having to dress and make our bed in a very few minutes, made the first morning seem like being dropped into the bowels of hell itself. This would be our morning routine, minus the trashcan banging, for the next several weeks. It was going to tax me both physically and mentally, in ways that I'd never known in my life.

First of all, I had to get to know all the guys in our unit. There were all types, some to my liking and some not. I was a minority, in that I was a college guy with nerdy tendencies, and a reader. I sensed most of the young men were more outdoorsy than me, were more physically fit to endure what we'd have to go through, and were still younger than me, many being in their teen years. The younger ones were actually gung ho to fight somebody. And then we had to figure each other out, since some of us were white Southerners, others African-American, others big city types, and others corn bread Midwesterners. Then we had Catholics, Jews, Baptists, evangelicals and the unreligious. We had shy guys, simpletons, smart asses, uncouth, mean and gentle souls. It was a collection of humanity, little of it martial, and our drill sergeants had to mold us into some kind of a fighting team, where we could think of ourselves as part of the union, not outside of it.

I was taking in this amalgam of humanity and wondering how I would fit in. I was still a civilian at heart. After all, I was almost 23 years old and had been a college student for four years. I had been dealing with what I had to do in school at my own speed and on a mostly solitary basis. I would be solitary no more; I would go at the speed expected by the Army, not my own. I was going to have to find new ways to cope, or I'd find myself in more trouble than I already was in.

As the weeks went by, we struggled to catch on to the Army way. It was tough going: early to rise, work like hell all day, and early to bed. We learned to march in step, do drills, handle the rifle, learn new rules and regulations in class, endure gassing, do kitchen duty in the mess hall, learn to shoot weapons and keep our areas organized, our barracks clean and learn to do what we were told, with no questions asked. It was an exercise in stripping down our individuality. If one of us failed, we all failed, more likely than not. When the drill sergeant at the processing station had told us to "be all for one, and one for all," he wasn't kidding. Punishing us along the same lines was highly effective. None of us wanted to be at fault and cause our buddies to lose out.

The training exercise that brought me down was not the running and marching since I was rail thin, but tests of upper body strength. The monkey bars turned out to be my nemesis. Before each meal we were supposed to jump up and grab the steel bars and swing along on them hand-to-hand from the beginning to the end, about 18 feet in length. Our feet were dangling three feet off the ground. On my maiden try, I gripped the bar and began the left-to-right swinging motions with my hands, all the time supporting my full body weight. In short order, I felt a ripping of the skin and a burning feeling in my hands. I endured it through a few more swings, and then dropped down. My hands were a bloody mess. My soft skin had been torn open by the pulling.

The drill sergeant was all over me, seconds after I fell to the ground.

"Hey, what's wrong with you, soldier? Get back up there, right now!"

But when he saw my bloody hands he knew I couldn't go on. He yelled at me to stand aside. I was humiliated, especially when I saw the country boys fly from one end to the other. No doubt, their hands were long ago callused by outside labor. I had not done much with my hands except push a pencil or pen for years. Now, I was paying for it, and everybody could see my weakness.

After a few days staying off the bars, I tried it again and my hands ripped open again. I was allowed to bypass the bars to allow my hands to callus up, so I had to run around them as before for a few more days. This was humiliating, since everybody else was doing the exercise, a requisite to entering the mess hall for chow. I did not like standing out in this way, not at all. While I hated the whole experience, I couldn't help but want to do better. My desire to improve, for the first time, was not just for my own benefit, but because I didn't want my failure to reflect badly on my squad. I was buying into the team mentality, despite myself.

Speaking of the all for one and one for all mentality, it was put to the test with our group on Saturday morning when our squad was denied the afternoon off because one guy had dusty boots. We all had worked our butts off shining our boots for inspection. We thought we were in good shape, but this lout had obviously been lazy about his own boots. After that, we did not let up because we had done our own work; instead, we checked on each other to make sure we looked good as a squad. It mattered, we were discovering. I had always been a lackadaisical person in general. My indolence hurt me in school, for sure. I'd study at the last minute, write term papers by doing the least I could get away with, and I was apt to drop classes I didn't like, and make good grades mostly in what I did like. I was into instant gratification, but my new circumstances were making it hard to stay the way I used to be. I had nowhere to hide, anymore. Now, I had to perform thoroughly because I was affecting other people. This was stressful, but it was also making me concentrate more. We couldn't flee; we had to do things we were loath to do, but still did them, anyway. There was no way out.

One Saturday morning I was assigned to cut and pull the weeds from a long row of shrubbery. I had to do it by noon or I could not get off for the afternoon. We cherished the rare free time that we could earn, so I was anxious to get the weeding job done. Free time meant we could go to a post canteen, goof off or play pool at the recreation area on base. Free time was precious because we could forget our struggles for a few hours.

So, I began the work, but as I looked at the long row ahead of me, then realizing it was about 9 o'clock in the morning, I couldn't see how I'd ever finish by noon. I was demoralized. But I went ahead with the work—again, what else could I do? I drudged on and on and on. And then something marvelous happened.

I finished weeding the whole row of shrubbery with about five minutes to spare. The drill sergeant looked it over, nodded his approval and told me to get the hell out of there. I complied with great joy, running down the road toward the recreational area. As I was in route, I looked back on my work, and felt a joy I'd rarely felt. On a primary level, I had simply done a mundane chore. But I had done more than that because I had exceeded my expectations for myself. This sense of accomplishment was a new, refreshing feeling for this well-intended, but under-achieving, young man.

My strategy for staying out of trouble in basic training went pretty well most of the time. I was always working to be inconspicuous. It was as if I was a civilian captured in a prisoner of war camp. In a way, I was, as a draftee. I was comforted, a little, because a few of my new friends felt the same way. But most of the guys were buying in, not only by their work, but also by their enthusiasm and sense of competition. A few of us were simply faking it. We did well enough and stayed out of trouble, but our performance was a form of passive resistance. We were always grumbling about the Army, criticizing the way we had to do things. I doubt we were helping the esprit de corps by our slack attitude. Yet, we were smart enough to stay out of trouble, and we did not purposely do anything to hurt our unit. We were resisting the reality we were in, surely, but we were not anti-military, per se. Despite our petulance, we were buying into the Army way more than we knew. But more instructive things happened to teach me when to comply and when to stand my ground. On my first day pulling kitchen duty (KP), I was sent to the rear of the huge kitchen to peel potatoes. I was given a small potato peeler to use, so I set about to do the work. Naturally, I was peeling the potatoes at my speed. After a while the sergeant came by, stood next to me, stared at me for a while, and then said to me:

"Damn, you the slowest motherfuckin' potato peeler I've ever seen. Ain't you ever done chores before? Pick it up, boy."

I was shocked at his mouth. I'd never heard a black man yell at me this way either. This was 1970. I was used to blacks treating me in a kindly, even deferential manner. In the Army now, I was seeing blacks in authority and they knew how to use their power. I had seen a black sergeant bless us out on the very first day, but most of his venom had been directed to the black recruit, not the white guys. But this black man had leveled his hostility on me. He did not like me. He did not like my work. This was man-to-man, not white against black. The military world, as I was discovering, was one where rank was the boss, not the color of one's skin.

With regard to doing what I wanted to do, as opposed to what I needed to do, I was used to going with the former instead of the latter. But I was learning. I had to admit, the sergeant was right. I was the slowest potato peeler in the world, and I knew it, because I could go faster, much faster, but I had not wanted to, and I got called on it. I was just being lazy, but to be caught at it put me to shame. I grumbled some, but picked up my speed.

I got another character wakeup call when a few of us soldiers were left to wash a jeep. We had more than enough to get the job done. We had about eight guys, a couple of water hoses, towels and rags aplenty. The drill sergeant left the task to us to do as we wanted. He said he'd be back in thirty minutes. Without supervision, we began to joke and stand around, while a few jumped into doing the job. I thought the guys doing the work by their own initiative were lackeys to authority, as much as I thought anything of them.

Then the drill sergeant returned. He looked at the squeaky clean jeep, and nodded his approval. Then he turned to us and told us to form a line, so we did that. Then he inspected us. I was thinking: *hurry up, man, I want to get back to our barrack*. He kept looking at us, casting his inquiring eye at our boots and pant legs. He then signaled to the guys who had been doing the work to take their leave, but indicated for the rest of us to remain. *How did he know they did the work?* I thought.

"You guys want to know why you are still here and why you all will be washing another jeep and picking up trash this afternoon, while those guys are off? It is because their boots and their pant legs are wet, while yours are dry. You were screwing around and let those guys do all the work. They are the good guys, you are not. Listen up, you're a good guy when you do right when nobody is watching, now ain't you?"

Dry boots! He got us good. I again had a hard truth thrown at me. Not by my mama or my high school teacher, or even by the politicians I admired, but by this hard core drill sergeant. Again, I felt ashamed. I had been called out on my craftiness. I was full of resentment against the Army and the military in general because I was here by coercion, not choice. I felt the institution was up to no good, so being shown up by a drill sergeant, who I still felt superior to, was unsettling. Again, on the ground, and far from the overarching crimes I assigned to the military, I was learning new lessons about responsibility and about being a team player. I was learning I had some growing up to do when it came to being a team player. *Damn, I wish I'd thrown in to wash the jeep*, I thought. The fact that I had stood there pretending I had worked, poised to be released from duty the same as the guys who had earned it, deeply embarrassed me. But it was too late now.

Then, there were times when I got it right and the Army came up short. My character wasn't totally depraved, and I had my moments.

My next challenge came about this way. We were on the parade grounds and there was a mass of soldiers lined up all around me. I was at the front of my line, which was comprised of about fifteen soldiers. The drill sergeant had ordered us to fall in after the line of soldiers going by us. When the soldiers did pass us, I wasn't sure if it was the correct line to follow. I hesitated to move and then decided to wait. The other line passed on by and without our line falling in, a gap was created between our line and theirs.

I had guessed wrong.

The drill sergeant stopped the whole show. All the assembled soldiers came to a halt. There were a few hundred guys now looking at the approaching drill sergeant and me. *Oh, shit, what now,* I thought. I was standing at attention, scared stiff.

The drill sergeant squared up, hands-on-hips and gave me the evil eye, if I ever had seen one.

"What's your problem, soldier?" he asked.

"I wasn't sure I was supposed to move out, drill sergeant," I said.

"I told you to move out after the line had passed you by."

"Well, I just thought…"

"That's the trouble, dumbass, you tried to think."

"Right, drill sergeant."

"You know what," he said with a raised voice, noting he had a captive audience. "You know what; I don't think you have a dick, that's what I think. Yeah, no balls for sure."

"Well, uh, actually I do, drill sergeant."

He looked really cross now. He didn't appreciate my smart ass answer. "Oh, you think you have one, well, I don't. I'll tell you what, pussy; pull it out if you have one. Let's see it." I could hear some snickering in the background. I glanced around and saw everybody hanging on our every word. I could feel sweat beads on my forehead. I resisted the urge to wipe them away. I also resisted the urge to ask him, if he was determined to talk about my private parts, to refer to it as a penis instead of a "dick." But I knew that would not go over well at all.

"Well, come on. Let's see if you have a dick or not," he bellowed. "Pull it out, right now!" This was a direct order, it would seem. I decided at that point that I'd had enough.

"No, sergeant. I don't think I can do that."

"You don't have one, then?" I remained silent at that point, and did not make any move to unbutton my pants. I was not going to let this degenerate get the best of me, no way.

There was an impasse.

Then the drill sergeant continued to stare me down, but his eyes seemed to have a slight twinkle in them. Maybe, he felt I had some steel in my spine, after all. He stepped away and waved me on. He had had his fun. He saw that I was not going to fall into his trap.

"Follow that line, boy, and get out of my sight," he screamed. I took off in a flash then and caught up with the line of soldiers in front. I wasn't that embarrassed. I thought he had embarrassed himself. It is in the rules that a soldier doesn't have to obey an illegal order, and I had refused to obey one that was certainly beyond the bounds of human decency.

Another time the drill sergeants tried to mess with me was when we were marching along somewhere and I was directly behind a soldier, Louie, being harassed by the drill sergeant. Louie was fat, not unheard of when the troop supply was coming from draftees. This guy had been struggling since day one. He was ridiculed for his weight all the time. He often had to do extra pushups and run extra distances due to his weight. It was no different on this day and on this march. The drill sergeant was leaning in on him.

"Pick it up, man. You are disgusting. Stay up!" Louie replied, "Yes, drill sergeant." This abuse kept going and I was largely tuning it out. I had heard this exchange before, but then the drill sergeant hurled a new insult, one I hadn't heard before.

"I say, pick it up, boo-boo." *Boo-boo*? I thought, snickering out loud. The drill sergeant heard me, jerking his head my way. *Oh, no*, I thought.

"What you're problem, Malone," he said.

"Nothing, drill sergeant," I said.

"You think this is funny?"

"No, drill sergeant."

"You don't think it's funny. But you're laughing."

"Yes, drill sergeant."

"You think it is funny, then?"

"No, ah, no, drill sergeant."

"Then you must be smiling because you like me, right?"

"Yes, I like you, drill sergeant."

"You like me!" he said, enraged. "You like me?" He got close to me, his breath smelled like sewer gas. "You queer, boy?"

"No, drill sergeant."

"No? But you said you liked me?"

"I do, drill sergeant."

"Then you like me. You want my Big Johnson, right?

"No, no drill sergeant."

"You don't like me?"

"Ah, ah." I fell silent.

Having reduced me to silence, he looked satisfied and marched on ahead. Louie glanced back at me. I gave him a quick smile, both of us mentally exhausted by the drill sergeant's dallying with us. But we shrugged it off and kept going. As the targets, we didn't realize that the exchange might have been more purposeful than it seemed. We were both stronger in our heads than we had been before. We suffered mental anguish, but we were sharper upstairs as a result. If we were ever to be captured by the enemy, and be subjected to their questions, we would be tougher than if we'd never faced hostile exchanges with authority we couldn't walk away from.

At long last, I completed basic training. I was never gladder to leave a place in my life as I was the State of Louisiana. I had my fill of big, nasty red ants, pine trees and pine straw, hot dry weather, old wooden Army barracks, and training grounds as flat as the wide fields of eastern North Carolina.

Thank God, I was out of there and basic training was done. I couldn't believe that I had survived it as well as I did. It wasn't that I was very strong, or very fast, or very smart, but I was strong enough, fast enough, and smart enough to see my way through a situation alien to me. I learned that I could do more than I imagined doing things I didn't like to do. And when I found myself in situations not of my choosing, it didn't mean I could disregard what I needed to do. The old adage, "bloom where you are planted," came to mind.

7

And as I sat waiting for orders in Saigon, still fresh from the road trip from Long Binh, I felt the "bloom" adage still held true, now more than ever.

More troops arrived; we joined another group of new guys, increasing our ranks to about thirty soldiers. We were told to wait there until further notice. I saw "hurry up and wait" was still alive and well, even in a war zone. We waited for about an hour, sweating under the intense midday sun.

"Wonder where we're heading?" a soldier from Alabama said. The guy next to him was from up North and replied, "Try Saigon. We're here, dumbass."

"Shut up, Yankee boy," the Alabama kid said, glaring his way.

"We're supposed to fight this war with the likes of

you?" the Yankee soldier said with a sneer.

"Hey, want some whup ass? no charge," the Alabama boy said.

"Sure, douchebag."

"What'd you call me?"

Both soldiers got to their feet and began to approach each other, ready, it seemed, to settle the Civil War all over again.

"Knock it off, here comes the sergeant," an older soldier, with an air of authority, said. We all looked up, but stayed put on the ground.

The brewing confrontation between North and South came to an abrupt halt. The sergeant first class walked up and told us not to get up. We were pretty pooped, drained from the long stay in the sun, so we were happy to oblige. We were anxious to get to our assignment. We knew it would somewhere in Saigon, of course, but there were various locales we could wind up in, some better than others. We were quiet now and listening.

"Okay. Any you boys know how to type? Raise your hand," he said without ceremony. None of us moved or raised our hands immediately. *Is this a trick?* I thought. *Does he really want a typist or not?* I pondered it and decided to take a chance. Thanks to my little high school having few course options, I had taken two typing courses just to graduate. I could type up a storm, actually.

I raised my hand.

My hand was the only one raised.

"What's your name, soldier?" the sergeant first class asked.

"Malone, sergeant first class." I called him by his rank insignia, which I had memorized by now.

"Sergeant will do, Malone."

He gave me a hard look, sizing me up. "So, you can type?" he said.

"Yes, sergeant. I took typing in high school," I said, trying to hide my anxiety. He continued to stare at me for a while, and then he looked to see if anybody else was available. It was just me.

"Get your belongings and come with me, Malone. The rest of you stay put," he said.

He turned and began walking to a small screened-in annex. I grabbed my stuff and followed him. Sweat was running down my neck, partly because I knew every man there probably despised me at that moment. I didn't look back, figuring I might get a single-finger salute from my compatriots.

I got inside the screened-in office and the sergeant told me to sit in a chair to my left. I did this and saw there was an old Underwood manual typewriter in front of me.

"All right, son. Let's see if you can really type," the sergeant first class said.

Another senior looking guy came up, too, and they were both leafing through my personnel file I gave them. This was my big chance, unless I screwed up the sudden audition. My hands were sweating, but it was from nerves, not the weather. I hadn't typed a word in months. But I put the paper in the machine, cracked my knuckles and went at it. I was asked to type a simple memo, and I proceeded to do this. My speed and accuracy came back to me naturally, just like riding a bike. I finished it up quickly. Both men looked at my work, glanced at each other, and seemed to be pleased enough. But I wasn't sure if I was going to be accepted or not. Heck, I was still marveling at being in a shaded area and not outside broiling under the sun with the group I'd just left behind.

Then my opportunity turned into a miracle when another soldier came walking in. It was my old buddy from MP school, Jim. He yelled a greeting to me, ran over, and we had a quick guy hug, followed by a handshake.

"Fellas, this is Charlie Malone. He was in MP school with me at Fort Gordon. He's fine." That was all it took. I was in. *Hot damn*, I thought. I could not believe this luck because I had not had any idea where my friend from MP school was assigned, except he was in Saigon somewhere.

Within the hour, I was assigned to the Provost Marshal's Office in downtown Saigon. Our billeting would be in the downtown area, as well, not on a military post proper—all of which were located on the outskirts of Saigon. Officially, I was now assigned to the 90th Military Police Detachment (Provost Marshal

Section (a.k.a. Chief of Police for Saigon), 18th Military Police Brigade.

I was tossed on a jeep with a staff sergeant named Jones, who had also been assigned to the Provost Marshal post. I didn't think I'd like this staff sergeant, a middle aged guy about to burst out of his uniform due to his heft, as well as I had SSG Shepherd. The traffic was still scary, but we got going and soon enough we screeched up to an old, shabby looking hotel with two guard posts out front. This was to be our living quarters. *Holy smokes*, I thought. *A hotel?* Soon enough, however, I found out it was no four-star affair. It was, indeed, the Capitol Hotel, US Military BEQ (Bachelors Enlisted Quarters) on Dong Khanh Street in the Cholon (Chinese) District of Saigon. I shared a room and bath with two other soldiers. I was on the third floor of this six-story building, which I soon found had no hot water, but did have lizards big as rats running up and down the walls and cockroaches big as mice racing around the floor. When I looked out of the window I saw the street below was paved, but full of potholes. There were women nearby sitting listlessly on straw mats and selling their wares, such as soft drinks, cigarettes or little bottles of gasoline. Yet, the street was teeming with heavy traffic: cars, trucks, bicycles, motorbikes, cyclos, and carts going to and thro. *This is so bizarre,* I thought.

Then I thought about the grunts in the jungles who had to fight off leeches and snakes, and, worse of all,

CHARLES MALONE

North Vietnamese Communists ready to kill them, and I shut my mouth. Considering the alternative, this old flophouse looked like the Waldorf Astoria. It also caught my attention that our new home was totally cut off from our Saigon military base twelve miles away, and except for the two guards out front—a duty I would be sharing soon enough—we were totally surrounded by about three million Vietnamese, few of them that friendly, and thousands of Viet Cong (communist insurgents). It would seem our safety depended on the good will of our neighbors, few that I wanted to come calling.

Despite my misgivings about the war, I knew I needed a weapon fast, and I asked right away about getting armed. Funny how that adage that there are "no atheists in a fox hole," was close to my thoughts on that first day, which were: "I may have my doubts, but it won't matter if I am dead." Soon enough, I did have an M-16 assault rifle and plenty of 20-round ammo magazines. The rifle was adapted for semi-automatic, three-round burst, and full-automatic fire. I was going to be a full-fledged soldier, after all. The surprise was that the terrain would be in a city, not in the jungle.

So, I joined the ranks of the Saigon based military police community. Along with my clerical work, I also had some street patrol duties and extensive courier responsibilities, which would have me driving from downtown Saigon to the MACV (U. S. Military Assistance Command Vietnam) headquarters next to

Tan Son Nhut Air Base across town and back daily—about twenty miles round-trip. I also had to pull periotic guard duty for our billet. It was a mixed bag of jobs, for sure.

On the surface, I had a sweetheart assignment. But accurately accessing the dangers within Saigon was like peeling away layers of an onion. Things were not what they seemed, and one had to develop a practiced eye for trouble. Troops in supporting roles in Saigon got in trouble when they developed a false sense of security because they were not in the boonies. This laxity made it easier for the Viet Cong, who were skilled at causing trouble in the least suspected places and by all means necessary.

The first week there we were briefed by our Command Sergeant Major, James Wilson, about the risks we faced in our urban surroundings. To make his point, he showed us a black and white glossy print photo of two MPs who had been murdered in a Saigon bar a few months before we had arrived. One was a sergeant and the other was a private first-class, both from C Company, 716th MP Battalion, who had responded to a report of a drunken soldier in a bar. They were shot dead by an ARVN (Army of the Republic of Vietnam) airborne commander, who had formerly guarded the Vietnamese Presidential Palace. No charges were ever filed against the ARVN officer.

I read another report about an American MP from the 716th MP who had a hand chopped off by a machete wielding major of the ARVN Rangers, during a bar fight in Saigon.

By1971 we were beginning to have increases in the number of "combat refusals," which was when American troops refused to obey orders they thought were illegal or suicidal. Everyone knew we were getting out of Vietnam. We knew the ARVN were lackluster fighters, so why should we take the risks, soldiers would ask. Incidents of "fragging" were going up, too. "Fragging" became an all-encompassing term for American troops shooting or grenading American officers who had ordered them out in the field. The soldiers usually felt the missions were suicidal. Regardless of motive, however, fragging and combat refusals were illegal and subject to court martial.

Other crimes by soldiers that MPs had to enforce included common criminal activity such as theft, black market activities, drug dealing, and violence done on each other (bar fights, mainly). And the old reliable of going AWOL—absent without official leave—was the crime of choice by American troops. I saw a lot of these prisoners in the detention center that was located directly below our office at the Provost Headquarters. Any American soldier arrested in Saigon usually stayed at our detention center for a few days before transfer to "LBJ," aka, Long Binh Jail. I had heard we had about 10,000 prisoners there.

Our detention center was nothing but a cage, part under cover with one commode, and the rest an open courtyard with high walls topped by barb wire. There were no amenities, just a concrete slab to sit on. Since the prisoners in our keep were so transient, we paid no attention to them. I wish I had given them a nod once-in-a-while. After all, they were still Americans, even in their state. But being in a war zone atmosphere, even in the rear, tended to drain away some of the common decency we'd learned at home.

8

The Saigon scene was extraordinary. There was a sea of people, both friend and foe. Who could tell? I heard a cacophony of languages spoken daily, saw races and colors from all regions of the world, especially in Asia, and saw Americans of all kind in a new light. I was especially taken with the dramatic role of African-Americans in the military, not only with the new self-assuredness of the common black soldier, but from the actual authority held by the higher ranking blacks. I was liberal minded, but I was stunned by the transformation, because I had rarely seen blacks in authority. I had lived in a mostly white world, and had known blacks mostly in subservient roles. It was old habit, despite my feelings to the contrary. I was the product, despite my good intentions, of growing up in a small, provincial town in the South. But I was up for the change. I knew I'd been on the right side of history since my early days when I met racial reality head on. I couldn't forget it. My education began with Adam when I was eleven years old back in my hometown of Coats, North Carolina.

The phone rang loudly, like a falling metal pot hitting a linoleum floor.

We all flinched, since it was too late for a call that was up to any good. My father slowly picked up the receiver and quietly said hello - as was his way - and then listened patiently. In the meantime, we all, including my mother and two brothers, sat anxiously on our stools around the kitchen bar, afraid that bad news about Adam was on the way.

"Hmmm, all right, bye," Dad said, again slowly putting the receiver down. He sat there, took a long drag on a cigarette, let the smoke blow out through his mouth, then through his nose. He looked around at each of us with teary eyes. He let out a deep breath, obviously dreading to tell us what he'd just heard. Finally, he said, "I'm afraid Adam didn't make it. He's dead." Our worst fears had become reality.

My mom let out a soft cry, looking flushed with grief. We three boys were stunned. I started crying. Being the youngest at eleven years of age, I could still cry without embarrassment, unlike my older brothers, Johnny, thirteen, and Teddy, fifteen. We had never known anybody to be murdered, until now.

Two days before the dreaded call, Adam, an elderly black man who had worked for over 30 years for our family along with his wife, Queenie, got his head bashed in by another black man using a wooden chair. The man had been provoked when Adam walked up to his front porch, where he was severely beating his kids, and told him he shouldn't be hitting his children like that. The belligerent father immediately turned his rage on Adam, grabbed a chair, and plummeted him on the head and back with it. Adam fell back off the porch onto the front yard, where he was later found lying there in a heap, bloody all over from his head wounds. It probably didn't take much to knock him down: Adam was a frail, elderly man. He had not been looking for a fight on that fateful evening; he had just wanted to stop one.

When the assailant was finished with Adam, he turned on his heels and ambled back inside his house, slamming the screen door behind him and returning to his supper waiting on the kitchen table. His family gave him a wide berth, for they didn't want to be next on his hit list. Adam was simply left to lie there in the front yard. At some point, somebody called the law. There was no hurry, considering it was two old blacks going at it on a Saturday night in the colored section of our small town in rural North Carolina. The police finally got there and arrested the attacker, who hadn't even bothered to run away, and took him to jail. Adam was taken to the local hospital, his condition critical. Good thing that this hospital, at least, had a section for people of color, not always a sure thing in those days of racial segregation, known as Jim Crow.

Later that evening, the police contacted my dad, since it was common knowledge in our town that Adam once worked for him, and still hung around us if there ever was any work to be done. Piddling work was about the only kind Adam was able to do anymore. But my dad was a kindly fellow, and just wanted Adam around. Yeah, my dad, Elmer Taylor "Ted" Malone, was big-hearted, and my mother, Mildred Winborne Malone, was also not disposed to make Adam do anything more than be our surrogate parent. After all, Adam had helped to raise her, too. We Malones were known to have a soft spot for "coloreds" and that made us seem "peculiar" to some folks in the neighborhood.

Upon hearing the news about Adam had been attacked, my dad gathered all of us up and we sped to the hospital. I don't recall anybody else showing up but us. God only knows where Adam's wife Queenie was, what with her drinking and tuberculosis condition making her nearly home bound with a relative down in the "bottom," which was the name for the area where blacks lived in our small town. Adam used to complain to us that the worst thing our maternal grandfather, John Edgar Winborne had ever done to him was to make him marry "that woman."

Many years back, Granddad had found out that Adam and Queenie were living together in a common-law relationship in a back room of the small grocery store "Mr. Edgar" ran near Bailey. Co-habitation in those days would not do. He put Adam and Queenie on a train for Dillon, South Carolina, a popular locale for quick civil marriages, gave them money for fare, plus a twenty-dollar bill wrapped around a bottle of whiskey to celebrate the occasion, and ordered them to not come back without a marriage license. And they tied the knot in short order.

Adam and Queenie were not slaves, of course, in the legal sense, but old traditions of subservience had not yet died out in the 1920s, which was about the time this act of benign mastery by my grandparents over Adam and Queenie took place. Where ever my grandparents lived, they were there to serve them. When my grandparents had no more work for them, they simply took up with my parents. By the time I came along, Adam and Queenie were no longer working exclusively for us, for we had little money or much work for them to do.

Anyway, I was scared to death as I drew near Adam's hospital room. Walking in there, we saw Adam lying on a bed, his face laced in bandages, tubes running out of his nose and all sorts of appendages attached to him to monitor his feeble and gasping efforts to live. He never spoke, or responded to our pleas. "Is he going to be all right, Daddy?" I asked.

"I don't know, son," he said. "He's hurt pretty bad."

"Adam, please, don't die!" I cried. "Adam, come on, come on, please say something to me!" I drew closer to him and held on to his arm, but he didn't move a bit.

"Come on, Charles," my mother said, putting her arm around me. "Let's go and let Adam rest some."

We all left and made our way to our car in the parking lot.

"Quit crying, Charles" my brother Johnny said.

"Shut up," I replied, wiping the tears from my cheeks. "Just leave me alone."

"Crying won't bring him back, you know."

"I know, I know. Just leave me alone, okay?"

"Fine, little brother, fine, I'll leave you alone," he said, flicking my ear as he rushed to get into the back seat of the car. I tried to swat him back, but he evaded me by a hair.

"All right, boys, that's enough," my father said, all the while lighting up a cigarette. I was always amazed by how he could talk and dangle a cigarette from one corner of his mouth, all at the same time. We rode home in near silence.

Our hopes and prayers for a miracle were extinguished by the dreaded call to our house the next evening. Adam was dead.

We went to the funeral a few days later—all, except my dad, who had to work, and Johnny, who had to be somewhere else for reasons I forget. I was nervous, for whites to go to a black funeral, or a black anything, was unusual in those days. This was 1959 and Jim Crow (legal segregation of the races) was still alive and well.

But my mother thought it only natural to go and pay respects to a man who was instrumental in raising her. That is how far back old Adam Oakes went with our family. He even taught me how to ride a bicycle. He had simply taken off the training wheels one day, put me on the bike and pushed me off down the road. I pedaled for all I was worth before wobbling around and crashing into a ditch. Adam put me back on the bike and pushed me off again, and again, until I got the hang of it.

And I also remember him taking me to the movies. I squawked about having to sit in the balcony and not down front, but he told me to "be quiet." I later realized the movie theater had been segregated in those days and blacks were allowed only in the balcony. Adam was too sensitive to my feelings to share that bit of reality with me. Adam also took my brother, Teddy, to the segregated area of the theater. In later years, Teddy would recall that he threw popcorn down on the white people below, much to Adam's chagrin. He would giggle and yell out cuss words from the upper perch of the theater.

"Hey, you niggers keep it down up there!" the white people below would yell back up to them. It was all Adam could do to hush Teddy up. He didn't want any trouble. I think he had an easier time with me.

Anyhow, my mother and grandmother were old school Southern ladies, who could not abide missing any funeral they had the slightest justification to attend. Why else did they scour the obituaries daily with a devotion to detail that would rival the planning of the D-Day invasion of Normandy Beach?

At the funeral, several ladies from Adam's family greeted us cordially. They were dressed mighty fine, all topped off with fancy hats, matching handbags and jewelry. They made over my mother, who was decked out pretty well herself. She beamed from the attention. I was shy and followed her, along with my older brother, Teddy.

But before we sat in the sanctuary where everybody was gathering, I got to see Adam in a side room. He was laid out in all his splendor in an open casket. With everybody else socializing, I was left there alone, just Adam and me. I stared down on his peaceful face, eyes closed. I marveled that his head looked normal, no a scratch to be seen. I wondered how the undertaker had worked such miracles to make him look presentable, but then I really didn't want to know exactly how the ghastly work had been done.

Seeing Adam there, I recalled when I was once forced to touch my grandfather, who lay in a casket in the living room of the Malone homestead in Bear Grass, N. C., a few years before, by a well-intentioned aunt, but upon touching his hard, ice-cold face, I had flinched in horror.

But now I cried in earnest. I said my good-byes and then some. I couldn't believe he was gone because I'd never known anyone to die by the foul hand of another person. I had seen old folks die by natural causes, and while it was sad, it was the natural order, of things. *Why, God? Why?* I thought. The mystery of God's ways never seemed more alien to me than at that moment. But, oh, do black folks know how to send a departed soul away, or what? Adam was rolled out in front, right under the pulpit, all showered with flower bouquets, sprays, and wreaths. The roses, lilies, and hydrangeas created a sea of pinks, yellows and lavenders. My senses were hit like a two-by-four by the pungent fragrance of these many flower arrangements. So, we settled in for the ceremony. Poor, distraught Queenie was led in by a group of "nurses," all dressed in white. They were armed with Kleenex, the weapon of choice for all the crying ladies. The people down front to the right were from Adam's family. They kept their distance from Queenie, who they looked down on. They had shared with us, while we were outside before the service, that they felt Adam had married beneath himself. They felt that Queenie's sorry ways had slowed him down.

Mother had the good taste not to bring up the inconvenient fact that her father had forced Adam and Queenie to get married. I learned from this exchange that class snobbery was not the sole property of white people. Lord knows, my mom had her nose high in the air, constantly making snide remarks about this person or that. She was always on the lookout to find out if people were from the "wrong side of the track." Yet, she was a contradiction, since she always acted kindly toward people of color, somehow placing them outside her social boundaries, or perhaps beneath them.

The funeral proceeded. It was a fascinating celebration of life and of faith, of a sort I'd never seen in my own staid, white Baptist church. The music started up with a thumping organ melody, rising and falling in sync with the preacher's voice. After the opening remarks, the hymn, "Swing Low, Sweet Chariot," was done up-tempo, and a multitude of voices chimed in to make a truly "joyful sound unto the Lord." Some called this a "shouting church," but to say a service such as this one was only shouting didn't do it justice.

As the music picked up in its intensity, the only person in that room not swaying to and fro was poor old Adam, lying there still and at peace, in front of everybody. The preacher then got up to give his eulogy for Adam. He started slowly, calmly, and quietly drew us all in to his welcoming rhetoric. He spoke of the good deeds done by Adam, and of what a fine family he came from. He deftly mentioned Queenie in a neutral light before he went on to explain how Adam was on his way to a better world, to Heaven, in fact, and was "glory bound and at rest on those celestial shores." I liked the vision, but felt I wanted to wait a long, long time before it was my turn to land on those "celestial shores." And I bet everybody else was in agreement with me. I figured everybody wanted his or her sins forgiven, but not just yet.

Then, the preacher pulled out a handkerchief, wiped his perspiring forehead, took a deep breath, and let out a shout that startled me, causing me to swallow my chewing gum. "Praise Jesus, my brothers and sisters! Repent of your sins, on this day!" the preacher shouted.

"Our departed brother, Adam, is safe up in Heaven, for he was a humble soul." The preacher eyed everyone in the room, looking slowly around. "But what about you...and you...and you?" He was pointing his finger left, right and center, zeroing in on those there that probably needed prodding the most. I could see them shrink down a little each time that old finger pointed their way.

But the sermon was getting me excited, even if I was also afraid. This stuff was not at all like our preacher, who was always so calm and, well, so dull. Where I went to church, the clock spoke louder than the preacher, but there was no clock watching here. We were too busy "hearing the word," old time religion style.

By the time this preacher was finished, he had torn into us so much that we almost wished we could tag along with Adam and get the whole thing over with, poor sinners that we were. And then he had us go up front to give a "love offering." Stern deacons stood there with baskets to take in the loot. Mother gave a dollar, and my brother and I gave some coins, which was all we had.

So, grand words were said about Adam, the Lord was glorified, the people were given due warnings to stop sinning, and then we finished with a lively version of "I'm Going Up to Heaven, Anyhow."

One of the reasons we felt Adam's loss so badly was that we had previously decided to bring him with us to live on the beach. We were planning to move and work there running an apartment house on the ocean front. My mom and dad were going to fix up a little annex for Adam to live in, so he could always be on hand to help Dad do the maintenance work necessary to keep the place functional. It would have been easy work. Adam would have loved it there, we felt. We were also amazed that this new move was on the horizon, thanks to our dad screwing up the courage to buy the old place and run it, all the while staying with his probation job. My dad was always working hard, seemingly caught between doing public work for his soul, and finagling on the side to make enough money to survive. We knew, however, that this gig was sending us all to live on the beach. Who really works on the beach?

"Halleluiah!" my oldest brother said to me. "We're

moving to the beach! Girls, sand, swimming, just everything!" Being almost sixteen, Teddy had a different meaning than I did for "everything," but I got the general picture.

The apartment house my dad had bought was on the ocean front. It was three stories high and contained fifteen apartments. It had a colonial look about it, with its tall front porch columns, and white clapboard siding. Facing the ocean, it had a wrap-around porch where people could relax in the numerous rocking chairs, sipping their drinks, smoking their cigarettes or just gazing at the surf and sea. Each apartment had a small kitchen with a gas stove, living area and one or two bedrooms. In those days, there was no air conditioning, so each dwelling was ventilated either by fans or by opening the large screened windows to let the winds flow through, as well as the accumulating sand. At high tide, the waters would come up just under our front porch, so we had an up close and personal view of the ocean. In later years the local civic leaders wisely constructed a large berm up and down the Wrightsville Beach coastline that set the sea back by at least two hundred feet, saving the island for future generations. This newly found island and our place in it was idyllic; it seemed like a world away from the rural, farming community we were leaving behind.

We were overdue to leave our hometown in Harnett County, considering the restlessness of my father, and the discontent of my mother. For both of them, having been in Harnett County for over ten years trying to scrape out a living had taken its toll. As far as the old families in Harnett County, not to mention Coats, were concerned, our family was a new breed. Since my parents had moved there as adults, they were considered transplants. We were seen as "outsiders," even after ten years living there. To be really accepted in this county, one had to be, at least, second generation. Our family was not ostracized, by any means, and we had some dear friends, but insider status just took time in the slow environs of a rural area. Of course, as a child, I had no realization of this kind of social stratification. Coats was the only home I'd ever known. It was a big deal to leave it, as far as I was concerned. But, looking back, it was less a big deal for my parents to pick up and leave, having done this type of thing before.

My father was restless, to say the least, and ready to move and take advantage of the beach house opportunity. As risky as it was to take up the big mortgage, plus hold on to the house we already lived in, he had to be chomping at the bit to go. No doubt he was spurred on by my mother always talking down where we lived, and, by extension, belittling my dad for his "stupidity" to bring us to Harnett County. Mildred was an ex-city girl, who had never forgiven my dad for removing her from "civilization and to this God-forsaken place." When she was in a bitter mood, she would remind us of the advantages she had had living in either Wilson or Greenville, both towns much larger than the two-stoplight town of Coats.

She would eventually grow to like our hometown, but that was not the case in our formative years. Since her maturity level was always a work in progress, she instilled in us a feeling of inferiority about our upbringing in Coats. And, regrettably, she also embedded in us a bit of snobbery about ourselves in relation to our neighbors. My father paid no attention to her airs, but we kids were a captive audience.

We had begun to envision a new life on Wrightsville Beach, North Carolina. We were heading there for the next summer, if we could stand to spend one more school year in Coats. My mother was caught up in the excitement of moving to a new place, or so it seemed, at first. We loved it when she was happy because nobody was more fun than her in her good moments, and nobody was more miserable than her in her bad moments.

My father was always the steady, calm and quiet one, but when Mildred was on the warpath, he tended to take off and leave us on our own to face the music. In retrospect, and to be fair, perhaps she was bringing up unavoidable topics that he was choosing to avoid. He was the risk taker, after all.

Regardless of which parent was in the right, my father's advice about our mother was to "not take her seriously." "She is spoiled," he said to us. "She will get over it, so just baby her." He would gather us into the kitchen around the bar, usually after some kind of dust up in the house, to give us advice about life in general. These serious meetings were always held out of earshot of our mother. Still, when she was on a prowl, he always had an option denied to us boys, which was to simply walk out and drive away somewhere.

Saturday was our cleanup day at home. We had a special way of handling it. We would awaken in our upstairs rooms to a wailing and bemoaning voice, Mildred's voice:

"How did I ever come to this? I have nobody to help me. This house is a mess. The floors are dirty, the trash is full. But nobody does anything, but me!" Then she would cry out, and the banging of kitchen cabinet doors would begin, or the clanking of pots and pans.

"My sons don't love me. Nobody loves me! Why? Why?"

"Shit," Johnny said, as he pulled himself out of bed. "We'd better get down there and start cleaning. She won't shut up until we do."

Teddy was still in his bed across the upstairs hall from our room, trying to ignore it all, but we rousted him out of his bed to get down there like us.

"Hey, Teddy, get the hell up! We're not going to do it all," Johnny said, shaking him to get moving. Johnny was the middle brother, and he was always the first one up, first to do his chores and first in about everything else. Teddy was the slowest, ever the poet and intellectual, and I was somewhere in between.

"All right, I'm up," Teddy said, rubbing his sleepy eyes.

"What'd you do, Teddy, stay up all night playing solitary?" I asked.

"None of your business, Charles; get out of my room."

He slammed the door so he could dress.

"Naw, he was playing with himself," Johnny said, as we both laughed.

We could hear Teddy making angry snorts, since his door was closed, so we just got busy ourselves getting dressed to go help Mom clean the house up. This was the usual Saturday routine, always preceded by Mildred's pity party. We boys had our own assigned chores, and mine was polishing furniture, which I actually liked to do. There was something satisfying about seeing dark wood go from dull to shiny. I could see the effects of my work right away. Teddy cleaned the floors and windows, while Johnny cleaned the bathroom and swept the outside deck.

Usually an hour or so into all of this activity, we'd begin to hear our mom hum a melody of some kind, sort of a sing-song, up and down thing. That was our signal that she was pleased, and we could get the hell out of there. We didn't expect a direct thank you for our help, but we didn't care; we just wanted to leave. Johnny and I were most likely to be found at our local high school gym, playing basketball through the afternoon. Teddy, however, would probably find a private place to read, draw or play solitaire.

With the new adventure looming, however, Mother was pretty happy and that meant more play time outside for us, better food and more trips to Raleigh to buy clothes. The only shadow on our improved prospects was the sad fact that we would not be able to take Adam. We had never considered bringing Queenie, who was estranged from Adam.

Naturally, Adam would have agreed with that decision. The word was that after Adam's funeral, Queenie had holed up somewhere in the Bottom, living off the charity of neighbors and often falling into a state of dereliction. Now and then, when Queenie would show up at our door, always asking for something, Mother would fuss her out, but would usually give in and give her some food or money to help her get by.

We were able to find out about Queenie's shenanigans because of our black maid, Nellie Lee, who came once a week to do our ironing, was a great source of information about who had done what and to whom. Mildred liked her ironing, but enjoyed more her gossip about her friends, and more deliciously, gossiping about the white folks in town she also worked for during other times of the week. Nellie was memorable to me because she always told the truth about things. She was never malicious and also displayed an enormous amount of common sense. I learned a lot from her during our talks in the kitchen, usually when I came home from school and was getting a snack while she was there ironing. Today, people would say Nellie was never my friend and was only performing in order to keep her job and not upset a white person. I will never believe it was that simple. Yes, many blacks put on an act to survive, but there were situations where blacks and whites genuinely got along. We were all constrained by the times. But people of different races did have confidences and quiet friendships with each other, such as we had with Nellie Lee.

A few months after the murder, the old guy who killed him got a plea deal orchestrated by his lawyer: only two years in prison.

"Damn, is that all," my father said, when he heard about the deal. He was angry. As a probation officer, he was familiar with the courts, lawyers, judges and the whole rigmarole. "If I got caught stealing a ham sandwich, I would get that much time."

"Daddy, why did this man get only two years in jail? Just that for killing Adam?" I asked. I was dismayed by the obvious injustice. Slumped in on my stool at our kitchen bar, I hung my head down, slowly moving my head left to right and back, fighting off yet another bout with crying. But Johnny was sitting next to me, gloomy over the news.

"I mean, don't people get life in prison, or the electric chair, for murder, Daddy?" I continued, staring at my dad with genuine puzzlement in my eyes, all so innocent about the reality of this situation.

"Well, I reckon I can figure it out," he said.

"How come such a light sentence,?" Johnny asked.

"Boys, Adam is a black who killed another black," he said.

"He wasn't just a black, Daddy, he was Adam!" I cried.

"Adam, to you, son, but just an old colored man to bout everybody else."

"But this ain't fair to Adam, even if he is black," Johnny said.

"Well, boys, you all are right. It ain't fair. You got to learn everything in life ain't fair. This is one of them," Dad mumbled, feeling uncomfortable admitting to anything that would lower our respect for the rule of law and order, unequal as he knew it was.

"Adam was as good as anybody. It still ain't fair!" I said, not letting it go.

"I know he was. We know it, but the law is not always administered exactly the same in all cases. It's a thing called extenuating circumstances," Dad said, trying to explain more fully.

"Yeah, like happening to be a Nigger," I said.

Now, we were getting to the heart of the matter.

"Charles, don't say that word in this house," my mother said quietly. "We don't talk that way, you understand"? She had a hard look on her face I didn't like. I glanced at my father, who had a harder look on his face I definitely didn't like.

"But I hear it every day at school," I persisted.

"Me, too," Johnny said.

"Count me in. Some folks try to say Nigra, though," Teddy said.

"Or colored," Johnny said.

"Well, I'm serious. Just don't say the n-i-g-g-e-r word. I mean it, boys. We're not common folks. Only white trash uses that word," she said.

We all nodded in agreement, including our father. I got the feeling he had said the N-word while growing up on the farm. Yet, we all had said it now and then. But we knew it was wrong if our mother and father were so adamant about it. I decided to straighten up my language from that moment on.

"Look, boys, we can't bring Adam back now," Dad said. He stubbed out his cigarette. Then he stood up and laid his hands on the counter, looking like an earnest lawyer summing up before a jury.

"The sentence on this case is final, so let's just move on. I don't like it, either, but we've got a lot of work to do to get ready for the beach. So, let's finish up eating now and get to other things," he said.

We could tell by his look that this conversation was over. We were usually dodging Mildred, but on the rare occasions when our father got worked up over something, we jumped all the higher. My dad was never one to talk loudly or to show his anger or grief, so when he showed any emotion on something, we knew to get in line.

Our family packed up our gear and drove to Wrightsville Beach to begin working in winter to make it ready for the summer. The apartment house was a haunting place: dark interiors, empty halls, and rustic rooms, all in dark woods. There was a ground floor wrap-around porch and two small porches on the second and third levels, all ocean-front. We could hear the drone of the ocean throughout. It was cold too, and we shivered as we began the long, tedious work of cleaning the place up, which started with the never-ending job sweeping sand out of the halls and the apartments and the heavier drifts piled up on the porches outside. I wore out broom after broom during those early weekends.

My dad was all over the place, usually with toolbox in hand, fixing this and that. The gas stoves were often broken, electrical wiring in disrepair, windows broken, and beds in disorder: you name it. The place was a regal old barn, but it was, if the truth be told, in shabby condition. My proud mother soon became disenchanted with the place, due to its pitiful state. Mildred liked her comforts, but few were to be seen in this forlorn place. While my dad saw only the possibilities, she saw only the obstacles. Her mood began to grow darker as we spent each weekend toiling to ready the place for summer.

Of course, we boys, especially me, got to take off frequently and explore things. It was glorious to play with abandon on the isolated beach during the winter and early spring. We had our dog, Longfellow, a low-legged and long-bodied brown dachshund. He made us laugh by the way he would furiously dig at crab holes, trying to catch the fleeing crabs. His breed was bred to scent, chase and flush out, so he was madly happy to be in his element.

We also spent much time perfecting the art of throwing small seashells into the approaching waves. Certain shells, usually the long ones, could be held a certain way to maximize the curve to be applied to it. I pretended to be a major league baseball pitcher throwing a wicked curve to strike out Mickey Mantle for the great win. But being a huge Yankee fan, I more than likely dreamed of striking out a Giants player, like, maybe, Willie Mays. We would also play whiffle ball, which enabled us, due to the light weight of the plastic ball, and the winds of the surf, to throw extreme curves and drops and so on. We could run and jump and dive, never worrying about falling down, because the sand was soft and we rarely got hurt.

Then we might throw the football around. Our most dangerous game was to receive a throw, usually from Johnny—the best athlete—while running into the ocean. The thrill came from not being able to watch for the football and the incoming waves at the same time. It was likely that when the football was caught, immediately thereafter a wave would smack you down. It was good training for being tackled if in a real game. And what fun it was. We would run this exercise until we were exhausted, then limp to the apartment house, all wet and salty, and happy, as if this was the way the world should always be.

Mom had to call us extra times to get in for supper. And Dad would appear from somewhere, chores postponed, for a lively, chatty supper in our small, spare apartment. A game of Scrabble might break out, afterwards. Even our mother would relax and be content, if only for those cozy times we spent together holed up in our small apartment, protected by our little space heater, and the open stove door, if needed. We felt snug as a rug during those early times when we felt we had that gray, cold and windy island of Wrightsville Beach all to ourselves.

Finally, school was out and the first summer began for us on Wrightsville Beach. It was 1959. The apartments were fixed up and finally being rented out. My dad was becoming a little less anxious with rent money in his hands, instead of just bills.

The guests began showing up in droves. To our joy, many had young daughters that we Malone boys could check out, as if they were there just for our picking. There was a new batch of guests, or renters, each week, so we were meeting new people from what seemed like exotic places all the time. I'd never sat and talked to people from New York, Ohio or Kentucky, so it was not only fun, but socially expanding to interact with so many people, who often had a different slant on life. I found that my reflex of thought conditioned by my background was rapidly being reconstructed by my new horizons.

We were also doing a lot of swimming and body surfing. I was unafraid of the incoming waves, the bigger the better. And we were soon tanned as little bears, from head to toe. We were also snobby about being native beach people, as opposed to the tourists, who came and went. We also made cruel fun of the tourists with a farmer's tan, which meant a red neck and brown arms, but chalk white legs, who were tip-toeing over the broken shells and hop-scotching on the sand. As natives, our feet had toughened up to walk on any surface.

We also found that we couldn't play all the time, but had to help our parents do the things that had to be done for the maintenance of the place, and for the comfort of our guests. My special job was to keep all the trash cans empty. It was a smelly job, for there was no plastic liners back then, just flimsy newspaper, to line the cans with. All the while the cans were loaded with rotting food and all sorts of emitting fetid odors. I'd lug them down the steps and put them in the trash shed across the street in front of our place. The shed was located behind a white wooden lattice enclosure. With the fierce heat causing rapid decay, I was constantly using a water hose to clean the metal cans after the garbage man had picked the trash up on his regular runs.

But I was still happy because I was able to get in,

on average, plenty more hours of play than work. That was the benefit of being the youngest brother, a fact I took ample advantage of.

Wrightsville Beach was an incorporated town when we got there, and it still is today. It is located in New Hanover County and is just east of Wilmington. The town consists of a four-mile-long beach island, an interior island called Harbor Island, and pockets of commercial property on the mainland.

The most significant structure on the island was the Lumina Pavilion, which opened in 1905. In its heyday, it attracted numerous entertainers, including most of the famous Big Bands. My mother had attended some of the dances, back in her glory days in the 1930s. She got country club boys to drive her and her girlfriends there for a "gay ole time," as they used to say. No farmer boys for her, that is, until she married one: my dad.

Beneath a garland of red, blue and yellow party lights, hanging on the upper deck, I would watch couples dancing to such tunes as "16 Candles" by The Crests, "To Know Him is to Love Him" by the Teddy Bears and "Dream Lover" by Bobby Darin. My older brothers would try to get in on the action, but I was still too young to take part in the real fun.

I got my kicks from staying busy making my way around on the roller skating rink that had replaced the old dance floor. All of it—the din of laughter, dance music, pinball noises, and roller skating melodies rafting about, and the drone of the nearby ocean rolling in—attracted us like moths to a flame. And to think, Lumina was just a stone's throw from our place. We had it made.

When I was done with my daily chores at our apartment house, I took to visiting my new buddy, a black kid name Benny. He was the kitchen boy at the New Hanover Country Club, a large facility next door to our place. Benny was mainly a dish washer, but he could be found doing waiter duties or whatever he was called upon to do.

The New Hanover Club was always busy. The facility was three stories high, had several rooms to rent, plus the place had a spacious wrap-around porch. It had weathered grey-shingled siding with white trim that made it blend in the sea and surf, especially during a storm. Its dark, knotty-pined interior also had a large dining room where lunches and evening dinners were served to the club members and guests.

Benny and the other staff there had a lot to do, but he was always welcoming to me, for I was the only person close to his age for him to be friendly with. Benny was about two years older than me, and he loved to play the radio in that steamy kitchen, always hotter than the hot outside, what with the stoves burning and the steamy dish washing going on. I remember he was partial to turning up such songs as Fats Domino's "Blue Berry Hill," "Stagger Lee" by Lloyd Price, and some other stuff by Hank Ballard and the Midnighters, Jackie Wilson and James Brown. We'd both shake and shimmy some by the sink, and then straighten up when Mister Avery, the boss, came in. He was always shouting for Benny to do this or that. We exchanged quick glances, rolled our eyes, and I scampered out of there so he wouldn't get in trouble.

Benny actually lived at the New Hanover Club facility, as well. It must have been easier to have him there all the time; all the restrictions caused by segregation, which was alive and well at that time, would have affected his ability to come to work and get home again with impunity. So, he had a small room in the basement. Fairly often I'd go over there at night to just talk, listen to music, or to play blackjack.

Except for me, I doubt Benny had any friends, or was able to go much of anywhere. Yet, he was usually pretty up-beat, and he rarely complained. Of course, he knew it was unsafe for him to ever voice his true feelings to anyone white, even to me. But I could see he was getting restless, and bored. Heck, he couldn't even go to Lumina like us and play pin ball machines. He was not allowed to skate, or, certainly, take part in the dances there.

Benny was just a little black kid in a white play land; a place he well knew was for us and not for him. If Benny was out and about on the club premises, he'd damn better have a wash rag in his hand or an apron around his waist. I felt badly for him, but what could anyone do about it? And even worse, what could two kids do about much of anything that adults condoned, even stupid things like segregation?

Well, we did finally come up with one small, but significant, way to beat the system that kept Benny under wraps. It all unfolded in this way.

"Okay, Charles, deal me two more," Benny said, smiling slightly at his own hand.

"There you go," I said, handing them over. I slowly drank from my can of Pepsi. He was working his way through a Mountain Dew.

"Got ya, boy," he said. "Black jack, Jack! Give me my dough!"

"Man, you win all the time."

"Stay around me, son, and you'll learn to win, too."

And so it went for a while, just playing cards. Benny won most of the time, but I'd prevail now and then, much to his displeasure. He would make this funny, wrinkly face when I slapped down the winning combination of cards for a win.

On this particular evening, we grew tired of playing and were just sitting there. I wanted to go out somewhere, but I knew I couldn't take Benny. He knew it, too. We were two little friends against the world. I didn't even tell my parents I was his buddy, although I felt they were more likely than any white person I knew to like him. Why not? Hadn't we always accepted Adam and Queenie? So, we just sat there in silence for a while, staring out the little window, so dirty with caked up sand that we could barely see anything. It was hot, too, for there was no way for the breezes to get inside.

"Man," Benny said, "I'd love to go swimming. I'm damn hot and sweaty."

"Yeah, the ocean will cool you off, for sure." I dared not bring up the obvious, which was that only I, the white one, could go swimming. I supposed it was illegal for him to go swimming, but it didn't matter, for if he did go swimming, he'd get his ass kicked or worse, legal or not. Benny was well aware of this fact of life, too.

We pondered it for a time and as we did, our mood shifted from feeling helpless to one of wanting to do a little push back.

"Benny, you know what, why don't we both go swimming?" I said.

I was ready to take a risk.

"Uh, I don't know, man. It's risky, bro, but I'd like to do it, that's for damn sure," he replied. His eyes began to widen, and he had a grin on his face, at last. He was screwing up his courage to believe that doing this crazy thing just might be in order.

So, it was then and there that we decided to go swimming: the both of us, and to hell with what the big people thought. But we had to do a little planning for this excursion. We could not be caught, period. He had his job to keep, and, even more important, his good health to protect. I knew I'd get in a bunch of trouble, as well, for aiding and abetting in this full-fledged violation of Mr. Jim Crow.

At last, we figured we'd wait for a moonless night, so that we could sneak out to the waters in optimal conditions of darkness. A night or two later, we had our dark night. With the clouds covering the moon, the night was dark as burnt metal.

"Charles, you sure 'bout this," Benny asked, as he crouched low beside the club, looking high and low for anybody walking by.

"Sure, why not?" I said, blithely, not fully understanding the danger Benny was exposing himself to, as compared to me. I might get a scolding, but he could get a lot worse, if we were caught.

Indeed, the broad sandy beach was almost indistinguishable from the incoming tide, except for the reoccurring white crests of the waves. The ocean song was like the roar from a large shell held to your ear, more immediate than its distant drone heard from Benny's room. He had rarely been this close to the water, for his room, while 200 feet away from the incoming tide, and might as well have been 200 miles away. But the barn door was open now, and this horse was ready to ride.

We scanned the skies to find the moon, but we couldn't see any sign of light, just a few stars twinkling amid the streaming clouds. It was a pitch-black night, as was most of the ocean. For possibly the first time in his life, Benny was glad he had a dark complexion, for he did blend in well to the environs, even to where I had trouble seeing him if he strayed too far from me.

"See anybody?" I asked, trying hard to stay calm. My heart was beating rapidly.

"Naw, looks clear to me. Ready to go?"

"Yeah, let's go," I said.

Slowly, almost crab-like, we sauntered down toward the water. The sand was cool and cushiony to our feet. When we crunched a shell, we stopped dead still, for the sound was amplified to us by our fear. Then we went on for a few more feet, and then a few more, until we finally reached water's edge. It was low tide, our only miscalculation, since it forced us to cover more distance. But, at last, we were getting our feet wet. Our feet sunk into the sand and were washed over by rushing white foam. We then slid into the water and swam out, so to be as out of sight as possible. The waves were gentle, so that helped us to make our time in the water all the less conspicuous.

Up to our necks, at last, the salt water felt great. We began to splash around, laugh, and dive under to touch the seabed. We did this over and over. The current separated us, at one point, and I had trouble making Benny out because of the darkness. But his big smile and happy eyes shone through, almost like an apparition.

"Hell, yeah, man, this is fine!" Benny cried. "I didn't know you white folks was having so much fun."

"You really ain't been in the ocean before?" I

asked, amazed that so many places were closed to him.

"No way. I know of a black beach somewhere on the coast, but I ain't ever been there."

After about 20 minutes, we'd had enough and decided to come in. I knew my family might come looking for me before too much longer, anyway, and I didn't want that complication. We body surfed on an incoming wave and rolled up on the beach.

Then we froze where we lay.

"Oh, shit, man, there's Avery, my boss," Benny whispered to me. We were inches apart now, both of us lying prostrate in the foam, shells and sea weeds of the oscillating tide.

"You sure?" I quietly said.

"I'm damn sure."

"Where?

"Up there on the upper porch. Sum' bitch is taking a smoke."

I was momentarily stunned. Despite my liberal attitude about race, I had never heard a black make a derogatory statement about a white person. But I got over it real quick, considering my butt was on the line, too. I thought he'd tagged Avery about right, anyway.

"You know, Charles?" Benny said.

"What's that?"

"If you were black as me right now, we'd have a better chance to get out of this. You are shinning like a beached whale."

"Well, I can't do much about that now, can I?"

"I know. Crap! He's coming down the steps. Shit!"

Avery had flipped his cigarette away and was slowly coming down the steps. When he reached the bottom, he turn slightly to the right, looked about, then unzipped his pants and peed into the sand, just outside of the lady's bath entrance.

"What a dog," Benny said. "Look at that, right where everybody goes in and out, and him peeing there." But Avery's crudeness was our salvation. When Avery had finished relieving himself, he walked back around to the front of the club. With that move, we made ours. We scampered up to the back door on the bottom level that we'd left unlocked. Reaching the door in a rush, we quickly got back inside.

Mission accomplished! We didn't get caught! We high-fived and Benny went to his room and I went home to our apartment. We were not about to breathe a word. But Benny went to bed that night knowing he had swam in the ocean, as good as any white boy on Wrightsville Beach, and he was happy, if only for that one night. And I believe that his expectations for life went up a notch, just like any of us, when we experience a new thing, a good thing, that we had not expected to experience. For a lonely black kid to swim in the ocean when the reigning society of his time told him not to do so, made him believe customs were not static. I was a believer, too, after that happy night. I saw in Benny's joyous face our future, no matter the obstacles of that day.

9

During my first days in Saigon, I felt safe enough to travel on the main streets and to visit some areas downtown where a lot of G.I.s roamed. As long as we didn't stray off the well-beaten paths, the odds were that we would be safe. But our safety was never guaranteed and we always had to keep our eyes open, even when the crowds seem to pose no obvious threat.

The downtown streets crackled with energy. All the people were busily engaged in some form of survival or another. Activities ranged from vendors in little stands selling gasoline to food and drink, or to general merchandise. The merchandise was varied; some of it native stuff, but a lot was bootlegged American products, such as cigarettes, toiletries, military uniforms, sodas and electronics. We would see both modern looking Vietnamese women in western dress, even mini-skirts, as well as the popular traditional dress, mostly the colorful ao dai, a long dress that was a tight-fitting tunic worn over pantaloons.

The streets were crowded, noisy from the array of vehicles, mostly motor scooters and the mix of old European cars and military vans and trucks. When I rode, I usually took a cyclo—taxis that consist of a two-person carriage attached to the front of a bicycle. Riding was a way to get relief from the intense heat. In the South, the climate was sticky-hot year-round. I'd heard the North around Hanoi had winters that were chilly, gray and drizzly. But we never had changes in Saigon, always hot except for the monsoon season, when heavy rains would pour down without notice and then disappear just as quickly. I've loved summer rains ever since.

On the center square downtown I could see the Majestic Hotel near the banks of the Saigon River. Then there was the Continental Hotel built during the French Colonial period in the 1880s that had a wide veranda with overhead fans and tropical plants. A few times I sat there on white wicker furniture and was waited on by waiters with white coats and black bow-ties. I noticed that foreign journalists and businessmen frequented this place, while it was rare that soldiers, especially the lowly enlisted ones like me, would go there. I just had to sit there, even if it was for only a time or two.

The Continental Hotel was near the huge Saigon Opera House and was located on the corner of Tu Do Street, the main thoroughfare for the string of restaurants, shops, bars and bordellos that were the centerpiece for the downtown business center. Neon signs were flashing, American rock and soul music was blaring and Vietnamese party girls would stand and solicit American soldiers to come in and buy them a "Saigon Tea" and keep them company. The girls would sit with a G.I. and keep him company if he bought her a drink. The teas were pricy, but that was because the woman and her wiles came with the drink. It was cheaper to buy beer, alcohol or soda and keep company only with friends, usually fellow G.I.s that came in with you.

But being All-American boys, most of the guys wanted nothing more than female company during their time off. The bar manager made sure the soldiers were filling up the lady's glass on a steady basis, or there would be no more company. A few of the more enterprising bar girls would arrange for stays at their villas or for shared living arrangements, if the Americans or Europeans were willing to pay the price.

Not long after I had settled into my digs in downtown Saigon, I ventured out one evening to see what the allures of Du Do (now Dong Khoi) Street were all about. I walked by one bar, brightly lit with blue and red neon lights, where a cute little Vietnamese girl beckoned me to come over.

"Hey, come on over here. I give you number one good time."

I waved back and said, "Ah, another time."

"Hey, you must be cherry boy. You are new. Come on over for boom boom (means short time with prostitute) time."

I was embarrassed that she had figured out I was green as a hornet to the ways of the Saigon streets. As I made my way onward, she switched from being charming to being irritated, since I had turned her down. I heard her say with a huff: "dinky dau," which is Vietnamese for "crazy." And she called me "Cheap Charlie," for good measure. She was right about the last epithet.

The bar girls, the cyclo and cab drivers, the whole ragtag universe of street people, it seemed, spoke the pidgin English of GI slang. If things were good, they were No. 1. If things were bad, they were No. 10. The bar girls promised a bukku good time (from the French beau coups). Few American soldiers passed up the chance to spend time with these young ladies, some partially French—leftovers from the French colonial days, when their soldiers, obviously, had been concentrating on activities besides fighting Communism.

The girls of French origin, and later of American, who would be called Amerasians, were largely scorned by the indigenous Vietnamese. It was as if they were the face of the enemy, and these poor children were vilified to the point that the only viable place many of them felt they could get any attention, or even a bit of love, was from foreigners who welcomed their favors, even if for a price. I noticed the French-Vietnamese girls, many now in their teens or early twenties, as being beautiful. They had the straight, thick black hair of the oriental, but Caucasian facial features including round eyes, and white or light olive skins. It was incongruent to see them in their natural beauty, only to open their mouth and speak the crackle of the Vietnamese language. And they often were poorly dressed, often in rags, being the leftovers of the earlier unpopular war with the French. These women straddled two worlds, but belonged to neither. Many were abandoned and sent to orphanages, or sadly discarded in the streets by their shamed mothers. I heard they were taunted at school and made fun of because of their features. Their future, as Amerasian children would experience in future years as a result of the American presence, was to become waifs. Many of these girls lived on one great hope: escape to America and find their father.

It all seemed decadent on the surface, but these places were a short-term break for many a lonely G.I., where he could enjoy female company, music and an adult beverage. Of course, even these ventures could be risky. The soldiers who went wild when out on the town tended to pay a bigger price for their escapades than they had hoped to pay. They wound up being the victim of robbery, assault, shootings, or of being parted with much of their pay by false promises of romance by beguiling young ladies. While the street crimes were reported and showed up on our daily military police crime blotter, the incidents of trickery by the women went largely unreported. The victims were too embarrassed to make an official complaint and chalked it up to experience.

The nightlife in downtown Saigon remained strong until the Communists finally took the city over in 1975. The whole wild and wooly scene was nothing unique for men at war overseas. In fact, it was a time-honored tradition seen, for good or ill, in ports of call throughout the world for foreign soldiers. In its best sense, the social scene on Tu Do Street during the war years reminded me of the words from the song, "The Boxer" by Simon and Garfunkel, which had charitable words to say for the women of the night for the part they had to play in the mad, mad world of men at war and away from home.

Along with the night life in downtown Saigon, we also had Vietnamese hustling us to buy black market goods, ranging from illegal drugs—usually marijuana, or less so, heroin. Soldiers smoked pot to submerge their loneliness, or to screw up their courage to fight, or to just escape from reality. Of course, alcohol was a major drug of choice, and this was legal, to boot. I thought the Army aided and abetted the use of alcohol by offering it on bases at ultra-cheap prices, but nobody was complaining. I stayed away from "dope," but I had my share of beers throughout the year. I saw one guy, a sergeant, who was around thirty-five years old, turn from a casual drinker into an alcoholic before my eyes over the span of several months of nightly binges. Many a night we would carry him up the stairs to his room in our hotel. Amazingly, the man showed up for duty on time every day.

Also, to my amazement, we had a full-service bar in the lobby of our dumpy hotel, manned by Vietnamese who offered up mixed drinks for about fifty-cents and cold beers for a quarter. There was a sad little jukebox in the corner, often playing downer country tunes. It was sad to see the lonely soldiers in there, night-after-night, downing all that booze at rock-bottom prices, and their only company was other lonely soldiers. This was not a good mix for taking the higher ground in the struggle to survive the hollow duty that was the Saigon Commando's. Of course, we were all finding our ways to cope. Some guys had religion, others had a girl at home and others had drugs. It was all a less-than-wonderful aspect of the war atmosphere.

The other painful thing I saw, not just as a soldier, but as a caring American taxpayer, was the massive fraud and waste brought about by the ever-present black market. The generic definition of a black market or underground economy is the market in which illegal goods are traded. Its application in Saigon was everything from drugs to everyday products, such as soap, cereal, clothing, sodas, cigarettes or appliances—often goods sold by G.I.s to Vietnamese crooks who would in turn then sell it on the street to the public, often Vietnamese nationals, all at much higher prices.

The American presence in this city and country, along with our vast amount of material goods, drove the price of many commodities out of the reach of the average wage earner of Vietnam. If we were hated for anything by the people we were supposed to be saving in South Vietnam, it was our complicity in creating massive inflation in the country. Our purchasing power dwarfed the local buying power, ranging from what taxi cab drivers could charge American soldiers over the normal local fare, from restaurant prices and gasoline (another commodity often stolen from our bases by G.I.s and sold to conniving Vietnamese). It was an economic mess that drove the Vietnamese working poor into peasants, from an economic point of view. This economic power filled us all with a sense of omnipotence, in my view. Our adverse economic impact on South Vietnam contributed mightily to tearing its social fabric to pieces. An estimated four million men, women and children fled to the fringes of cities and towns. They were shunted into makeshift camps of squalid shanties, where primitive sewers bred dysentery, malaria and other diseases. Thousands, desperate to eke out a living, drifted into Saigon. The sight of the beggars and hawkers roaming the streets, pulling at us for money was almost medieval in nature.

The black market practice I saw firsthand was an enterprising soldier who went around and collected the monthly cigarette purchase allotment granted to each soldier. We would either give our allotment away or sell it for a small price, much less than the value of the monthly allotment of, generally, ten cartons of cigarettes. Let's say the conniving soldier was able to collect thirty allotments worth ten dollars each. He would have a value of three hundred dollars. He would then go to the PX and buy thirty allotments worth of cigarettes, and sell them on the street to a Vietnamese dealer for six hundred dollars, a one hundred percent markup. Then the dealer would sell the products to the Vietnamese public for even more of a markup. Thus, our negative impact on inflation.

It was natural, therefore, that the Vietnamese public began to resent our presence there, and these were not from the Communist ranks, but from the people we hoped would stay loyal to the South Vietnamese government. The local government, of course, maintained a blind eye to this criminal activity, mainly because many of the local government leaders were up to their neck in corruption themselves.

Since the war, it has been documented that the leaders of the South Vietnamese government were consumed in graft, ranging from the hoarding of American fertilizer to create artificial shortages that sent prices sky rocking, to South Vietnamese President Thieu himself who fled Vietnam with millions in gold in April 1975. These dark deeds drove the value of the South Vietnamese piaster to low depths and fueled an epic black market in currency. Too many American officials simply passed this vast corruption off as a cost of doing business. The depth and breadth of the underground activity surely soured the feelings for South Vietnamese for their own government, and certainly for what they saw as their foreign overlords.

I had one personal encounter with a thief: my staff sergeant on our MP team in the Provost Marshall's Office. SSgt Willie Jones would get me to drive him to the local commissary run by the United States Government. He had a buddy there who slipped him packages of steak, and even made ready-to-pick-up sandwiches for him, too, on some occasions. It got my goat when I figured out what he was doing. SSgt Jones would brag about his little scam, which made me all the madder. After the theft, his routine was to drop by the hotel and he would go to his room and put the steaks in his refrigerator. Not many of us had a refrigerator, so how he got that appliance is another question. Anyway, I became fed up with it after about the third trip.

"Sergeant, I want you to know I'm not happy making these trips for you," I said, tightly gripping the wheel of our van.

"Why not, Charlie? You can have some steak, too, if

you want. Plenty more where this came from," he said, chuckling.

"No, Sergeant, I don't want any of the steaks. It's wrong for you to do this stealing. It's not right at all."

"Stealing? Who made you the Pope?"

"I'm nothing but a plain soldier, Sergeant. Let me put it this way, I'm flat out not driving you to do this, anymore."

"The hell you ain't. You'll drive where I tell you, Corporal," he said, rounding his shoulders and putting on his official look. He was both angry and shocked at my defiance.

"Okay, Sergeant, let me put it this way. If you insist, I'll ask our command sergeant major what he thinks of your little food runs." His eyes rounded in fear at the thought of facing our indomitable CSM Wilson.

"Why you little dipshit," he growled. "You do that. I'll make you pay."

"Pay how, Sergeant? I know you haven't been promoted in twenty years. You're the oldest damn E-5 I know and if you get in one more scrape at this point in your career, you'll get a quick retirement. How am I doing?"

This scenario shut him up. He knew he was on thin ice. He had been a sloppy soldier for years. Sergeant Jones was scared of our command sergeant major, James Wilson. SSgt Jones might have begged Wilson for some consideration as a fellow black man, but he knew Wilson was a by-the-book guy who had risen to his prestigious rank through the toughest times for minorities to be in the service: World War II and Korea. Wilson was a hell of a guy and this poor sergeant did not want to try justifying filching steaks from a government commissary. SSgt Jones never asked me to drive him anywhere again.

I could tell the local Vietnamese were struggling to survive, even on the streets of Saigon. I was daily besieged by beggars and street urchins. I gave to a few but learned this generosity would break me if I continued. Lord knows I was solicited for drugs, booze, dirty pictures and sex all the time. American G.I.s were treated like rock stars by their hungry fans, to the point some soldiers went crazy over it and fell for every scam or solicitation. I heard the line was steady for soldiers getting penicillin shots for venereal disease. One guy in our office, it was alleged, had caught VD seven or eight times. I thought he should have had his head examined, but he obviously was never thinking with his brain.

One time, the driver for the provost marshal parked the assigned jeep for his boss in front of a local bordello. He left the jeep parked all night in this vulnerable spot, especially so since we always had a serious curfew for Americans beginning at midnight. So, American MPs, patrolling by after the curfew, saw the illicit jeep, and they had it towed away.

The next morning the provost marshal was left

standing when his ride didn't show up. At about that same time, the driver woke up and realized, to his horror, that the jeep gone. We heard the provost marshal had to call to pick up another ride to work. It was the talk of the unit when we heard about it. I had wondered why the provost marshal, a full-bird colonel, had stormed in that morning looking so angry. We never saw the driver again. I heard he got a quick transfer to the farthest away post he could be assigned to. I bet he was eye-ball to eye-ball with the North Vietnamese in no time at all. Oh, yea, if any of us screwed up, we were usually threatened with being shipped off to a real war zone, or to the jungles.

The sad part of the street scene was to see the Vietnamese who were in dire straits. I saw many crippled South Vietnamese Army veterans, often with untreated injuries, begging for money, often legless and with eyes missing, but having no way to survive except to beg for handouts. We saw children in rags and children raising children, it seemed. One day when I was in a market, a Vietnamese girl, about fourteen, came up to me and begged for money. I refused her as kindly as I could, even though she was holding a baby that had a grotesque, open sore on the middle of her forehead. There were a number of peasants around, so I didn't want to give to one and then be rushed by scores of others.

But then a small girl about ten years old came forward and began begging me for money, as well. She grabbed me by the leg as I was trying to leave. She would not let go and I found myself trying to advance on one leg while I dragged her with the other one. I knew this looked bad, so I relented and gave her a coin. She immediately let go, and I was finally disentangled. But, as I feared, the other girl with the damaged baby, rushed back and pleaded for money, saying loudly that I had given the other girl money, so why not her? The small crowd was becoming agitated, so I gave her money, too, and then fled before I could be accosted again. I didn't mind helping the afflicted and did so many times. Indeed, I had affection for them, but there was simply a limit to what I could do.

Even though daily life in Saigon seemed safe on the surface, dangers lurked everywhere. I compared Saigon to Belfast, Northern Ireland, when the Irish "Troubles" were going on. Anybody—man, woman or child—in Belfast could be caught up in the spontaneous urban fighting between the Nationalists—pro-independent Ireland—and the loyalists—pro British— at any hour, on any day of the week.

Our billet was under guard because we were located far from an Army base, and we had to have some level of defense if dissidents or guerilla fighters decided to attack our facility. We knew the enemy was all around us, lying low until they wanted to engage.

Inter-city skirmishes tended to be hit and run, not full-scale attacks. So it was when I was awakened one morning by the rattle of gunfire around our window and balcony area. My roommate and I leaped out of bed, grabbed our M-16s, quickly rammed a magazine in them, and rushed to the balcony. We saw two American MPs on the ground, both wounded by gunfire. One was lying still on the far side of the narrow parking lot, while the other was directly below our balcony, holding his stomach with two hands, writhing in pain. The attackers were out of sight. My roommate told me to stay put and cover him. He rushed below to check out the situation. He was a medic and was going to render help for them. I stayed on the balcony and scanned the perimeter with my weapon, ready to fire if need be. Oddly, being under attack had a calming effect on me. Not the calm that comes from relaxation, but from intense focus on the task at hand. My task at that moment was to cover my buddies and make sure no more harm came to them. My mind was blank to anything else. As my roommate ran from one fallen soldier to the other, I held my finger on the trigger of my rifle and only released my grip when help arrived in about fifteen minutes. The injured soldiers were taken to the hospital.

I heard the soldiers—both shot in the stomach—had survived. Who did the shooting was never determined, but the initial incident stemmed from an argument over a cab fare. At some point, the cab driver turned from being a benign servant into a hostile combatant, bringing out a hidden weapon to shoot both soldiers before they could react. The greatest danger we had as

American soldiers in Saigon was relaxing and thinking we were beyond danger, simply because danger in this metropolis was always veiled by normalcy, by politeness and by routine. It could all change in the wink of an eye.

Soon after the shooting under our balcony, I drew my guard duty assignment for our billet. I was nervous, but knew we all had to have our turn doing guard duty. This job called for staying up all night in front of our hotel and keeping watch on the surroundings from within the guard tower located just to the right of the front entrance. I had my M-16 and a stack of 20-round ammo magazines, about ten of them. It was a long and lonesome duty, but when midnight struck and I knew the curfew was on, my adrenaline went up, for I was under orders then to challenge anyone on the streets, American or Vietnamese, in the military or not. The only authorized personnel on the streets during curfew were American or Vietnamese MP patrols. We could radio in for help, if we needed it.

The street in front of me was a major road: Dong Khanh Street- and was surrounded by wall-to-wall buildings, mostly businesses and shops that went on endlessly. There was not a blade of grass to be found in this urban jungle. It was spooky being so quiet. The soft glow from the street lamps cast odd shadows about, contrasting the blackness of the alley ways that seemed to sit there like baited mouse traps ready to snap shut and release some kind of horror.

I couldn't get over the contrast between this nightly morgue and the roar of the day where this same street would be teeming with traffic and the sidewalks would be full of people, all creating a din of noise that mixed foreign chatter with familiar vehicular sounds ranging from engine speak to horns blowing and brakes squealing. I settled into my guard mode easily enough, but it was never a relaxing mode because I had to always be ready to react to any noise, especially after curfew, that could mean real danger.

And I couldn't help but think how crazy it seemed to be in this situation. I was the only person between the Viet Cong, if they so desired to make trouble, and about three-hundred American guys lying asleep in the hotel behind me who put their trust in me. My hands had never fired a weapon at anybody, not even to hunt for deer or rabbit or birds, nothing. And there I was like a solitary fisherman on a pier, waiting with my pole, baited, as this rifle is loaded, for a strike. What would people at home think if they knew how precarious our situations are, how much we are surviving by fate, not by our preparedness.

But I survived the Saigon night all right, thankful there was no trouble. I adjusted with each guard assignment, to the point where I anticipated the duty without alarm. The trick was to never get too comfortable with it.

10

As I continued to adjust to my routine in Saigon, from my courier duties, occasional patrols and guard duty, I realized my father had had to make similar adjustments during his World War II days. Although he had died when I was only twelve years old, he still influenced me. I knew he'd had a tough time, yet he never reverted to cutting corners or slacking off. He never "lost his religion," so to speak. I was trying to emulate him, even if it was a subconscious effort.

All I saw of my parents, unfortunately, was when they were weighed down trying to make a living and raise us three boys. But their lives were more than a sum of hard times. In the beginning, theirs was a storybook romance, and a time of high hopes.

My mother and father met in 1941 when he came over to her parent's house, where she was living, at the invitation of a friend of his, to see a litter of kittens. The little venture may have been carried out under false colors, but the kittens served as a good excuse.

"I heard some voices downstairs, after my mother let these young men inside, supposedly to see our kittens," Mildred recalled years later. She smiled at the sweet memory. And, prodded to go on, she happily did so.

"Well, I saw my friend, Clyde, and this stranger with him. He was so shy. But I do declare, he had the prettiest blue eyes I have ever seen on a man."

His recollection was less rosy, for when he saw her, her face was slathered with cold cream and she had curlers in her hair.

"I think he said he never wanted to see me again," she said. "He wondered what Clyde was trying to get him into."

Later on, her friend Clyde prevailed on my father to take my mother to the annual June German Ball in nearby Rocky Mount. This was a popular, big band affair, usually held in gaily decorated tobacco warehouses. Ted hesitated, but went ahead and agreed to take her. He showed up at her door with some trepidation. In recalling the meeting, he described it along these lines: "I knocked on the door, and her mama let me in. I waited in the parlor for a while and then she appeared. Not the girl in curlers and cold cream, anymore, but a princess. She was all made up, had on a pretty gown. I could now see her pretty smile and lovely eyes." He said he wondered how she could be the same girl.

They had a great time at the ball. It was one of those instant moments that can happen between two people, when they know they can share everything because they are thinking alike, laughing at the same jokes, reacting in the same way to what they see and hear. They know, in short order, what the other is going to say, before they say it. They clicked.

My mother told me later that when they were strolling around on the balcony inside the ballroom they came upon an empty baby carriage. They stopped to look at it. Then then my father turned to her, smiled a little sheepish smile, and said they might well "fill up" that carriage one day.

"Oh, I blushed," she said.

Until my mother met my father, she had gone out mostly with country club boys, many of them fun-loving and heavy drinking. She was almost twenty-nine, though, and had always resisted more than one offer of marriage. In the back of her mind, she knew none of those frat-boys would make her really happy. My dad was the poorest guy she had ever been serious with, but she knew he would make her happy for the long run, not for just a weekend.

So, Ted and Mildred started a whirlwind romance, but it was interrupted within months when the

Japanese bombed Pearl Harbor on December 7th, 1941, and like so many thousands of young men across the land, Ted was galvanized and sought to sign up for military duty. He was soon in the Navy and in July of 1942 was sent to the University of Notre Dame as an apprentice seaman for a month and then assigned to the Midshipman school at Northwestern University in Chicago where he would be until October of 1942. He was part of the United States Navy Reserve Midshipmen's School, known as the Navy College Training Program, V-7, which had been jump started by President Franklin D. Roosevelt, a few years earlier. The school's aim was to recruit thousands of naval reserve officers to command the vastly expanding fleet in preparation for the war effort. The majority of the junior officers who graduated from the schools were dedicated to operations in the Far East, known as the Pacific Theater during the Second World War.

Upon reading surviving letters from my father to my mother while he was in training at Northwestern, the University of Notre Dame, and while on duty in San Francisco, and finally from his ship in the South Pacific, one sees a frustrated man deeply in love with his wife. He had signed on with the Navy in a rush of patriotic fervor, like tens-of-thousands of other young men, but he was confronted with the almost overwhelming demands of being a midshipman cadet the Navy was in a hurry to train for warfare. He was desperately lonely and wanted to be home.

He was disenchanted with Navy rules and found the school incredibly hard. Yet, he was determined to survive his despised military life for which he had obliged himself. He was still aware, of course, that he had a job, albeit a small one, to do as part of the massive effort by America and her allies to save the free world from the forces of despotism. He had conflicted feelings, but in this he was like thousands of other lonely young men who were bravely, if not mournfully, manning their posts during the many engagements that would become part of the U.S. wartime role in the sweep of the Second World War.

Ted was kept busy in the summer of 1942 in the U.S.N.R. Midshipmen's School as a cadet in an accelerated program, yet when he was off, he soon grew bored with roaming around downtown Chicago, going to USO dances, or going to the movies. He wanted Mildred in the worst way. He wrote: "Honey, I just can't wait to get out of here, regardless of what may come...Stay sweet and remember that I love you with all my heart."

And in another letter dated August 1, 1942, he penned: "I can still see you standing there at the station in Wilson that Sat. afternoon, the 4th of July, when my train pulled away. I think that was the most uncomfortable feeling that I have ever experienced. God knows I could hardly stand it. Yet, the fact that you were there pulling for me and loving me just made me be able to carry on."

Later, the romance heated up from a distance as they furiously wrote love letters between Wilson, North Carolina, and Chicago, Illinois. By the fall, things had become serious between them.

Ted wrote in October of 1942:

"I couldn't keep you off my mind all last night and today. Not that I tried to because my dreams of you were pleasant. While going and coming on the train and bus, it seemed that you should be there beside me. Sweetheart, I love you so much that I just can't wait two more weeks hardly to see you."

Their correspondence from several weeks before indicated they were "engaged," but didn't know when they would marry, due to the precariousness of his status with the Navy. It was in October that they finally decided for Mildred to travel to Chicago. Ted wrote his brother Tim on October 18: "We graduate and get our commissions Oct. 30th or Friday week. The dance for the class is to be Oct. 26th and Mildred is coming up for that and stay for graduation. The dance will be a very elaborate affair at a very elaborate place, "The Edgewater Beach Hotel," and it will be something we'll both have to remember and enjoy. They have bands there like Woody Herman, and other nationally known ones and they put on a floor show and all that."

She traveled by train to get to Chicago. Throughout the fall they had been undecided on whether to meet or not while he was still in midshipman's school, so for her to actually set forth on the trip was evidence that they were determined to meet, no matter what the situation was. Mildred left the Wilson, N. C. train station without giving her doting parents much notice. They must have stood on the train platform waving good-bye to her with heavy hearts, even as she must have been on cloud nine.

But back in Chicago, Ted worried about every aspect of this impending marriage. Even the purchase of a wedding ring was a worry for him, as noted in the October 18 letter to Tim:

"I'm having a hell of a time trying to study & get ready to get married and all of that here in a great big city with no money and about to flunk out every day. I went down town this afternoon and wandered in a jewelry shop. One man told me that a nice wedding ring cost around 8 to 12 dollars. I thought that was pretty high (ha) so I went in another place and he said 45 to 74 was just average. I know damn well I wasn't in a dime store to begin with and I know so little about the mess that now I don't know what the hell is nice or nothing so think I'll wait and let Mildred buy the thing when she gets here. She suggested getting a wedding ring now and get the engagement ring later on. I couldn't buy one from a dime store now, anyway, but will have about 75 when I graduate. I don't know whether I'll be able to get home or not. Mildred said she would have about 150. We'll have to use that. If she doesn't bring it and I should get in a tight I might wire you for some if you think you could help me. If you can't conveniently drop me a note back so I'll know not to depend on you. (Same old Taylor, huh?)"

Ted was determined to have her there, even if he was unsure of his status in school. He was deeply worried about Mildred surviving the rigors of the big city once she arrived. He wrote to her just before she was set to arrive:

"My Dearest Sweetheart. That two bucks I just spent talking to you was spent the best any two I ever spent. I'm so damn happy now that I heard your voice that I just want to shout and sing. Ye Gods! I wish this week were over. I don't know how in the hell I'll ever get through the exams with so many things on my mind. I was lucky this last week and passed everything okay. May God let me do it again this week.

The room I have for you is at the Knickerbocker Hotel, 163 E. Walton St. I tried about 6 or 7 before I finally found one that wasn't already filled up, so when the clerk said that he had a room I could reserve I told him okay before I even found out about the price or anything. He said, however, that they gave service men a special rate, and that it would be $2.50 per day. That is a good price for Chicago.

He took your name so that in case I can't meet you, you can go there and tell them your name and the room will be ready for you. I didn't see the room but one of the boys up here is getting one there for his mother and he said the rooms were okay. It's just a small hotel for Chicago, but it's a lot bigger than the Chevy.

The R.R. Station that you get off from may be a good distance from the hotel, but if I can't meet you the best fit is to take a taxi to the hotel, anyway. The bill may run up pretty good, but it can't be much worse than Richmond was. If you can, please let me know the name of the station that you will come to as there are several here, and I won't know which one to meet you at, if I can meet you. I told you not to send your bag on ahead, but what I meant was not to send it to the hotel. Just send it to the R.R. Station and pick it up when you arrive and take with you in the taxi. I'm not trying to tell you how to manage, but up here they don't give a damn about giving service to customers like they do down south, and it might get lost."

Still a cadet, he was under orders to remain in the student dormitory on the Northwestern campus. Within a few days, they dashed to Saint James Episcopal Church in central Chicago and were married there by a local priest, along with the requisite witnesses. There was no family present. It was almost like an elopement, but it was wartime and they couldn't wait any longer. Much later in the marriage, following the Second World War, my father would dryly joke, noting the October 31 date of their anniversary, which he had married on "Halloween."

He hit a bump in the road during this time, however, when he failed to pass the navigation part of the Naval Officer Training program. Every course had to be passed to graduate. This must have been Ted's worst nightmare come true, especially since his fiancé was either in route or already there when he got the devastating news. With Mildred finally in town about this same time, and despite the setback, they married, anyway. He was in heaven when it came to his new marital status, but he was in agony over his suspension from the midshipman program. He had come so close to graduating that he went to work to be readmitted with a vengeance. I think Mildred being there gave him a second wind, not to mention having his lovesick heart mended to better concentrate on his studies.

His desperation to not fail at this time is seen clearly in this letter he wrote to the Chief of Naval Personnel, dated October 4, 1942: "I feel that I actually came so near completing the course that if given another chance I could complete it with much more thoroughness and efficiency....I enlisted in V-7 soon after we entered the war because I thought I could be of more help in winning it there, and although this delay in getting into action is the greatest disappointment of my life, I am more determined than ever to carry on as I started." The October 4 date of this letter reveals that he knew he was in a state of "delay," to put it best, and he carried on with marriage plans and the pending October graduation date for his class as if he were in good standing.

He was too in love to let his real situation get in the way of seeing Mildred, even if he was in academic trouble. He just saw it as a "delay," and he turned out to be right. The fact is that Ted and Mildred did get their big night out at the Edgewater Beach Hotel and there is a surviving photo of the grand event that shows them sitting at a table with fellow midshipmen and their dates at a table adorned with food and bottles of wine. She is shown with her hand over his hand, which is on her shoulder. She is smiling with a face full of joy, while he looks like he is in awe just to be there.

His pleas to be readmitted were approved by the powers that be, so he got the second chance he wrote to the authorities that he "was earnestly praying" for. He went back with a vengeance, this time admitted to the midshipman program at the University of Notre Dame, and from where he ultimately prevailed in May of 1943. With a new wife by his side, my father was able to concentrate much better and had much more time to study, if for no other reason he no longer had to spend countless hours writing home to his sweetheart.

My father was sent to the South Pacific, following a brief time in San Francisco, finally seeing real sea duty. He rarely spoke of his role in these battles to liberate the islands in the Pacific. I cannot recall him telling us any war stories about those days. The Guam and Bougainville assaults were both fierce actions that saw thousands killed in days. My father was in charge of the organization and execution of amphibious landing and salvage of the landing craft, which was delivering the marines on the shore, so he was under heavy fire while he was doing his job during the invasions. The Japanese put up a strong resistance. He had to have the marines ferried in under enemy fire. The fighting was brutal and bloody, with over 1,700 Americans and over 18,000 Japanese killed in about two-weeks of intense fighting on Guam alone, according to published statistics of the engagement. These actions were intended to neutralize Japanese bases in the central Pacific, support the Allied drive to retake the Philippines, and to provide bases for a strategic bombing campaign against Japan.

He served on the U.S.S. *Libra*, originally built as a 10,000 ton merchant ship, according to the Naval Historical Center; it was "reclassified as an attack cargo ship in February 1943. The *Libra* continued to support operations in the Solomon Islands for the rest of that year, including participation in the Rendova landings in late June and the Bougainville invasion in

November. In 1944 and 1945, she carried cargo throughout the southern and western Pacific, and was part of the amphibious forces that assaulted Guam in July 1944, Lingayen Gulf in January 1945 and Iwo Jima a month later."

And while my father was quiet about his own efforts during those harrowing days in the South Pacific, his naval citation congratulated him for "excellent service in the line of his profession as Officer in Charge of a salvage party from July 21, to July 26, 1944, during the assault and capture of Guam. With professional skill and initiative, he ably assisted in organizing and controlling boat waves and supervised the salvage and repair of numerous damaged landing craft. Through his aggressive and courageous performance of duty, in the face of enemy fire, he contributed materially to the success of the assault operation. His conduct gives evidence of his great value to the naval service." The citation was signed by Admiral R. A. Spruance, the Commander Fifth Fleet, United States Pacific Fleet.

My mother said he was "never the same," after he returned. I think what the war did not take out of him, his post-war struggles chasing a dollar did.

My father's feelings and respect for Mildred—by now, his "Monkey"— during his time away from her, was ahead of its time. He did not want her merely barefoot and pregnant. He saw in her a full partner in their marriage, despite it being mostly a virtual partnership due to the vicissitudes of the war that kept them apart for almost two years. He wrote in 1943 from San Francisco:

"Monkey, I'm a long way from you, but I think of you constantly and have dreamed about 4-or-5 times about you. I do hope you are feeling better than you were and that you are getting along all right. If you ever need anything, or help, in any way you know who you can call on. It'll be hard for us to do much advising one another on questions that might come up, so I want you to remember this. Anytime, you want to do anything or make a change or anything, just do what you think is best. I'm with you whatever you do.

I love you, trust you, and believe in your ability enough to say that whatever you do is good enough. To me, you have proven that you are the best wife in the world and I feel lucky and thank God for you. You understand me and I do you.

This thing I'm in now is no plaything, Monkey. If I sat around and thought about it, it would be worse, so I'm going to try to have a good time. I don't mean a common or rough good time, but just something to be doing. You know that you are first, last, and always with me, so don't ever worry about what I might be doing. I want you to get out as much as you can because you'll feel better and time will pass faster that way."

Mildred was doing a good job of writing to him as well, according to his reaction to her messages. Tragically, none of her letters have survived. He saw everything she did with rose colored glasses. The farther away he was from her, and the longer he was away from her, only enhanced her being in his eyes. The only sour note in their correspondence was the fact that they had little money. He was constantly pressed to send her all he could, especially when their first child, Teddy, was born in December of 1943. The child was given the august name of Elmer Taylor Malone, Jr. I think it was Mother's doings to make Teddy a junior, but we don't know for sure. My dad never used the Elmer and went by Taylor in his youth. His first son would also eschew Elmer and was known as Teddy as he came along, until he graduated to the more serious sounding Ted as a young man.

In their letters, my father and mother had a lot to say about helping her parents out financially. They were both physically unable to work. Their declining health was a great cause of concern. My mother signed an affidavit attesting to the dire home situation on the 25th day of September, 1944:

"That her father, Adolphus Edgar Winborne, had a severe heart attack last October, (1943), and since that time has been confined to his bed two-thirds of the time; that he has been unable to do any work and has been under a physician's care constantly....that Affiant is unable, after diligent effort to obtain source of drinking water on her farm and, therefore, necessarily has to haul all drinking water to her baby and family from an adjoining farm, a distance of one mile; that Affiant's mother has arthritis in her hands and feet and is unable to help her...the Affiant moved to her farm from Wilson in the interest of her father's health and in order to help him. She has a colored man and his wife on her farm (Adam and Queenie) but they are totally incompetent and require close supervision...the Affiant further states that the responsibilities and duties connected with the farm require the close supervision of her husband."

In her own words, Mildred wrote: "The whole situation is becoming pretty desperate and there is no reason to believe that it will get any better. It is bound to be out of control before long unless we can get some relief in the form of management by an interested party. My husband is the only one that can furnish that relief, as I am the only child."

My father was frustrated because he could not help out at home more. As a result of Mildred's mother and father being unable to hold down jobs anymore, the home scene was precarious. My dad wrote in his letters of his desire to come home as soon as possible to help out, but he only took this tone following the epic liberation efforts of the Mariana Islands he was a part of during the summer of 1944. He hung on, returning to the States a few months later. He finally was given hardship consideration due to the family plight at home and was transferred to the East Coast in the summer of 1945. He was located close to home in Wilson, about 75 miles east at the Naval Air Station in Edenton, North Carolina.

Once back on American soil, he felt he was doing little good statewide, and wanted to get out quickly. It was evident the strain of being away from home while overseas, all the while knowing the hardships at home were piling up had taken its toll on his ability to cope.

During those days, the Navy issued reports "on the Fitness of Officers." My father had had good marks while overseas, including these favorable comments from his superior officer on the *Libra*: "The longer Ensign Malone is under my observation, the more impressed I am with his perseverance…. He conducted himself with credit during the recent combat landing in the northern Solomon's and during the two enemy air attacks… He is recommended for promotion."

Yet, when my father got back in the States and closer to home, he seemed to be a frustrated man as a result of being so close, but yet so far, from the beleaguered family farm, where my mother and her parents, and baby Teddy, were barely subsisting.

He began to slip on the job, based on the reports "on the Fitness of Officers" summaries during this period, i.e., "This officer lacks force and initiative.... In time, he should qualify for promotion." It appeared he was suffering from battle fatigue, felt guilty about not being able to help on the farm, and was experiencing letdown in his new job as the BOQ Officer, in charge of "the mess and officer's wine mess." He essentially ran the post liquor store. He felt his job was frivolous, especially compared with the serious duties he had had overseas.

The Second World War was on the downswing by middle 1945 and my dad felt like he'd done enough and wanted out, especially after the United States dropped atomic bombs in August of 1945 on Hiroshima and Nagasaki, Japan. The bombs were carried by a B-29 bomber, the Enola Gay that took off from Tinian, a North Pacific island in the Marianas, 1,500 miles south of Japan. The Marianas were opened up, of course, by the actions of the American forces my father had been engaged with.

My father came back a changed man, as were many of this generation of Americans, who, in President Franklin Roosevelt's words, had had "a rendezvous with destiny." In the words of author Tom Brokow in his iconic book "The Greatest Generation," millions of men and women were involved in the great adventure of the Second World War and had journeyed "through adversity and achievement, despair and triumph." My mother and father were would have identified with that characterization.

My father was finally discharged from active duty in late 1945, and he gleefully came home. Mildred was ecstatic to have him home full time and not under the control of the military. They were happy since he had been reassigned to the east coast after his Pacific duty because they had been able to live together for several months. By now they had two children, what with my middle brother, Johnny, being born in May of 1945. His Christian name was John Edgar Malone. He would go by Johnny, but assumed the more adult name of John once he got into college and thereafter. I came along in November of 1947.

My parents' joy to be at home together, at long last, and to be free of the Navy, was surely submerged by the new pressures of how to make ends meet. It wasn't just Ted and Mildred, carefree and easy, anymore. The family now included three small boys, each full of wants and needs. My father must have felt he had traded in one war for a new one, where the enemy was domestic bill collectors instead of the Japanese and Nazi fighters. My father simply buried his sorrows and his anger and soldiered on.

My father's hard transition from war to home mirrored the dilemma of many returning soldiers, sailors and airmen from war, including Vietnam, whereby the dream of home as a utopia disintegrated against home actualized. Like my dad, I held on to photos, letters, anything I read about North Carolina or about family, as special tokens of a place almost spiritual to me. I could not imagine home being a letdown. As the Pacific was to my dad, Vietnam was a place one could only get away from, not be from, or want to stay in. Since no power was stronger in sustaining our spirits abroad than dreams of home, it could be said that God was never wiser than when he prevented us from being able to predict the future.

11

If I thought I'd left behind the challenges of racial relations in America, I was mistaken. We all carry our ways with us, for good or ill, I reckon. I'd been astonished to see African-Americans behave in the Army with such self-confidence and authority. Despite my liberal attitude about race back home, I was like most typical white Southerners, and had rarely seen minorities act in any way except in subservience. White liberals had a magical belief that the black race would be forever grateful to be freed from segregation, and that would be the end of it. Not hardly.

When subjugated people are finally made free, it is a freedom to be fully human, or else it cannot be the real thing. And to be fully human is not to be humble alone, but to be all things on the behavior scale:

ambitious, conniving, aggressive, creative, loving, greedy, amoral, and so on ad infinitum.

For the first time, I saw the new liberation for African-Americans illustrated for me, not as a high-flown idea, but in the flesh; its practice mirrored people being people, really not just a black thing or a white thing, but a human being thing.

The military had been an unexpected laboratory since the 1950s to let black soldiers have the opportunity to live and serve based mainly on their rank, rather than their race. President Truman ordered the desegregation of the military by executive order in 1948, but General Matthew Ridgeway, leader of the United Nations Command in Korea, in 1953, gave the policy de facto effect when he successfully requested that his troops to be fully integrated, according to the Harry S. Truman Library archival records. Gradually, the military world created a haven for blacks to assert themselves and to reach positions of leadership far ahead of the norm in the civilian world. So it was in Vietnam.

I was surprised, but not unpleasantly so, to see that my immediate bosses in the 90th MP Detachment were black. SSgt Jones was a disappointment, yet even his brazen criminality was a mark of his self-confidence, self-serving as it was, and his desire to reach out boldly for what he wanted.

But Command Sergeant Major James Wilson was a black man who commanded respect, not only from blacks, but from whites, as well. Even the rednecks got in line for this man. In fact, CSM Wilson made officers sweat in his presence. He demanded the best from himself and all others. I once was out with him on day and a young white lieutenant passed by us and failed to return a salute given by CSM Wilson. Wilson stopped and turned around. He called out harshly to the young officer, who seemed to come out of a day dream before he realized who was calling out to him. It went this way:

"Lieutenant, did you not see me salute," Wilson said, still with his hand in a crisp salute, still waiting for a reaction.

The lieutenant returned the salute, kind of wimpy like, I thought, and said, "Sorry. As you were. Okay?"

Infuriated, Wilson leaned in to this piece of fresh meat and literally growled, "Lieutenant, you are my superior officer and I am duty bound to salute you, even the likes of you. By God, you will return my salute in a military manner. You have been honored to be an officer, as I am honored to be a non-commissioned officer, so you best return my salute like you mean it. And the salute of any enlisted man who honors your rank. Do you read me, sir?"

Shaking, the officer said he understood. He stood there, paralyzed in fear at this bear of a man with the voice of James Earl Jones. Then, Wilson saluted again, to which the lieutenant returned a much-improved salute, damn near knocking his cap off. Wilson then turned and we continued our walk. I could see a slight grin on his face, but he said no more. I thought this was an Army man through and through. I did not think of him as a black man first, anymore, but as a career soldier who lived and breathed his profession. I even felt some pride distilling into me, the ultimate draftee, because I was wearing the same uniform, if not rank, as this great man.

Back in the Provost Marshall's Headquarters, CSM Wilson would get on SSgt Jones as quickly as anyone else, if not more so. I think he wanted Jones to do well, but he went over backwards not to give him any preferential treatment, especially with all we white boys sitting around. One day, for example, Jones shamed a young white sergeant over some matter in front of the rest of us, including several Vietnamese staffers. When Jones was done, CSM Wilson, who had been silently observing this abuse of power, called Jones, the sergeant who had taken the tirade and me into his office. He then ripped Jones' head off because the staff sergeant had taken the sergeant to task—to the point of berating him--before the rest of us.

He told us to always take a man into a private area if we had to criticize him. And then he asked Jones what right he had to criticize anybody else considering the cock-ups he made. Jones said he had the right because he out-ranked the man he had been demeaning. Wilson said that was his first mistake. He said rank alone would not hold up if the power that went with it was poorly handled. This man had style, not just power. He did not just manage us, he inspired us, and that is what real leadership always does.

We were actually afraid of the CSM because he was such a stickler for the rules. I'd never seen a black guy assert himself in my past unless he was a preacher or a civil rights leader. I had seen blacks perform well, as athletes or entertainers, but not like this: in the ordinary world of doing important, real life things. In the years to come, I would never assume an African-American was not up to the job. I knew better because of my Army experience, and because of the example set by Wilson.

On the social side, Vietnam also made me take a new look at the rights of blacks to have all the fun they wanted, with whom they wanted. I'm talking about black men in bars with Asian girls. It wasn't so long before that I'd been shocked when a white girl got on stage to dance with a member of a black rhythm and blues band in North Carolina, but now I was seeing black guys sitting with pretty Asian girls, some partly French, happily buying them Saigon Teas, hugging and kissing them. None of the bar girls exhibited any hesitation to cavort with them that I ever saw. The hordes of white guys around seem to ignore it, even the Southerners.

It seemed absurd, in lieu of this new social order that I had passed up a chance to date a beautiful African-American girl, who'd befriended me while I was working as an intern on Capitol Hill in Washington, D. C. She was sweet, smart, just everything, but I was too scared to break the social code back home and take her out as was my want with any similar white girl. The sparks were flying for those precious first moments, but just as quickly died down when I remained fixed behind my desk in the Dirksen Senate Office Building. She stood at the door, gave me a sad look, said good-bye, and turned on her heels to walk down the marbled hallway and out of my life.

In Saigon, the local Vietnamese girls saw us all, black and white, as simply Americans. So, who were we to see it differently? If black and white soldiers were fighting and dying together, it seemed only right for them to seek their pleasures together.

We would all go home again with liberalized notions of what people are free to do: at home, at work and at play. Yeah, total freedom could be a mess.

Another dose of the new freedom hit me between the eyes one day when I was told I had two new roommates. I was ordered to get my stuff and go to their location. So, I got my gear and walked to the new room, knocked on the door and walked in. Sitting there were my two new roommates: one black guy and one Latino fellow. Both were very dark and foreign looking to me. I noticed we shared the same bathroom and our beds were barely a foot apart. The black guy stared at me and slowly leaned over and turned on his cassette player to emit a very loud rendition of "Psychedelic

Shack" by the Temptations. He was trying to aggravate me, or test me, I don't know. However, I must have fooled him, because I smiled and gave a little shake and told him I loved the Temptations.

Later on, I gave it back to him by turning up my James Taylor and Carole King tunes. Eventually, he admitted they were pretty good. We all found out we had more in common than not. The black guy and I often talked about Southern cuisine: butter beans, corn-on-the-cob, barbecue, fried chicken and so on. We had the same taste buds, for sure. But if the Army hadn't forced us to live together, we would have always stayed at arm's length.

The only time these two guys got to me was when they played a bad joke at my expense. They both burst into the room one day screaming that there were Vietcong coming up the stairs. Both of the guys ran into our bathroom and slammed the door shut. *What the hell?* I thought, suddenly seized with fear. I grabbed my M-16, loaded it, and jumped behind the door, ready to shoot the next soul who came through the door. I was crouching and holding a firm grip on the rifle when I noticed the door slowly open. They peeked out and got a look at me, all locked and loaded and poised for attack. They stumbled out of the bathroom and flopped on the bed, breaking out in hysterical laughter. It was all a joke. No Cong on the way.

"Dammit," I screamed, "I could have shot somebody!" I was hot, but eventually I laughed it off, too. We later went out for beers, and in their own way, by paying for a round, apologized. And there we were that evening, the ebony and ivory trio, just soldiers hanging out, and we were truer friends because we had survived our first falling out with each other. I was loosening up, despite my genteel Southern self.

Ironically, I found that the black guy and I had the same food favorites, mainly southern fried foods, such as chicken, pork chops, steaks and the high carbs such as mashed potatoes, butter beans, corn and black eyed peas. I teased him because he liked collard greens, which qualified him slightly more country bred than me. But to just look at this kid, so dark and menacing, I'd have never believed we had one single thing in common. He could have said the same for me, Mr. Whiter Than Butter.

And lest I come off as saying there was no racial tension in the Army and, in particular, South Vietnam, I would add that some white soldiers still enjoyed racial slurs and some black soldiers, influenced by the increasingly popular black separatist and black power movements, were parenthetically resentful of being in service and having to fight for a country they felt treated them unfairly.

The guys I was around—whatever their race—had issues with each other for any number of reasons. The ignition for a fight could come from stuff not purely racial, but also from differences of class, education, personality, political views and from plain old bullying or deceitful behavior. And, yes, sometimes a throw down would come because a black guy and a white guy hated each other's guts, maybe because of their race, and maybe not. Thankfully, I got along with everybody. And as for getting along with black folks, a couple of youthful experiences were etched into my brain that helped me along. My time as a busboy back on Wrightsville Beach was one of them.

I saw the civil rights momentum up close in the summer 1965 while I was working as a busboy at the Neptune Restaurant, an upscale place, on Wrightsville Beach. I had managed to finagle a summer job back at Wrightsville— now five years since we had left our beach apartment house. This new locale released me, at last, from the drudgery of working in the tobacco fields at home. I was enjoying working inside and being back on the island where our family had had its halcyon days, in my view.

It was a normal evening at the Neptune: crowded, noisy and busy. I was standing in the serving area, which was a partially closed in buffer between the kitchen and the open restaurant area that had both booths and tables. The place was not full to capacity, so there were a few empty tables up front. I was chatting with a couple of the waitresses, waiting to clean the next available table. At that moment, I saw four blacks, two adult couples, walk in; our hostess, after some hesitation, set them at a table. The whole place quieted down. All eyes were on this act of daring, or foolishness, depending on the point of view.

The civil rights laws had desegregated public restaurants, among other dwellings, about a year earlier, so these folks had the law on their side, even if they didn't have much social acceptance. I'd never seen blacks in a restaurant before that in a white restaurant. Most white Southerners had never eaten in an integrated establishment located in the South, myself included.

"Damn," one of the waitresses said, "I'm not serving them. Not me." She turned abruptly and stomped back into the kitchen, throwing open the swinging doors. That left two waitresses. "What are we going to do?" one of them said. There was confusion.

The hostess was glaring at us from the front. She was confused, as well. I don't know where the owner was at the time. Another minute passed, as the black group sat tight, quietly and pleasantly talking to each other, seemingly oblivious to the turmoil they had created around them. Yet, I could see them look over their shoulder, in quick glances, to make sure things were staying peaceful. Just because they had a legal right to be there didn't mean a redneck couldn't still break a beer bottle over their head. Another long minute passed. It was a standoff, and I was nervous as a cat. Finally, one of the waitresses, Phyllis, said, "To hell with it, I'll do it." She went to their table and took their orders. This one single act seemed to snap, like a cracking twig, the social norm of segregating anybody from the restaurant because of their race. The moment Phyllis laid down the menus, everybody knew the standoff was over. The white patrons did not want their vacation ruined by holding on to Jim Crow, so they shifted their attention back to their own table. They were more interested in their Jim Beams, as the host county was dry, and, surely many of the people had liquor in brown bags under their table.

The din of noise in the restaurant picked back up, laughter ensued, and when the black couple left, darned if they didn't leave a four dollar tip, way bigger than normal. As the busboy, I collected the tip and handed it to Phyllis with a grin. Phyllis got the last laugh that night. After that big tip, when the next black couple came in a week later, there was practically a fight to see which waitress could wait on them. Again, the pioneering couple left a generous tip.

So, green power and a good dose of bravery by these anonymous trailblazers helped break down the walls of segregation, and it seemed the local white business community, and certainly the tourists, were as happy to be free of the nuisance as were blacks. Privately, business leaders had conceded for years that holding on to these ancient prejudices had been bad for business. As it turned out, letting freedom ring also meant that the cash registers would be ringing, too.

The second influence to my diversity growth came along in the same year, 1965. This year was seeing more pressure from civil rights groups to advance racial equality, to enforce the anti-discrimination laws recently put on the books. If I had ever had any doubt about the morality of this movement, I got a boost of motivation by getting to attend a rally in Raleigh that summer featuring Dr. Martin Luther King, Jr. It was held at The William Neal Reynolds Coliseum on the N. C. State University campus.

Mother, oddly enough, wanted to go, so she got Teddy and me to go with her. While I knew she was generally agreeable to the aspirations of Dr. King, I suspected she was more motivated by a desire to show up her social rival in Coats, a liberal-minded lady professor, who was also planning to attend. My mother made a point of waving to the professor, who was singing in the choir, from our balcony seat looking down on the choral group and the stage where Dr. King gave the principal address. The high-minded professor looked shocked to see her nemesis showing the same social boldness as her. She could not claim to have sole ownership of the moral high ground, as was her want, this time around. While most of us were smiling after the speech by King, Mother was smiling beforehand, her mission being already accomplished.

There were about 5,000 people there, mostly black, with a scattering of whites, us included. We were nervous about being there, as was normally the case in those years. It was still unusual to have mixed-groups in a social or official setting. We also knew there was a corresponding Ku Klux Klan meeting at nearby Nash Square, protesting King's presence in Raleigh. But our nerves settled down as we were drawn to the noisy, joyous gathering. It was part tent revival and part political theater. We heard warm up speakers, including a flamboyant black preacher who passed the hat with the admonition: "It's not white power; it's not black power, friends, but green power!" Everybody laughed. But they all knew it was true.

We had to wait about an hour before Dr. King arrived. He was known to be perpetually late, but seeing him slowly thread through the crowd from the rear up to the front stage was akin to a presidential entrance. People were in ecstasy. The applause and cheers were ringing in our ears. We were all on the edge of our seats, all excited.

Then he began his address.

The audience was silent and reverent in the beginning.

Is this a sermon or a lecture? I began to wonder. He was moving slowly along, making good sense, but not arousing us. I had last heard an African American preaching at Adam's funeral, and this was not the same thing: no shouting, no appeals to our emotions. But I was judging only the first part of his sermon.

What I learned on that day was that Martin Luther King Jr. knew exactly what he was doing; he preached in the traditional African American style, which was to wind his way methodically, even melodiously, using well placed words, almost like poetry, all the while gradually upping the tempo. Toward the end of his address, he was speaking at full force and with high passion. His message, delivered in an authoritative, baritone voice, reached a final crescendo, calling on everyone to take action to build a better world.

I remember Dr. King said that nonviolent resistance was the only effective strategy for social change available to black people. He warned black youth against going along with the recent pleas by some of their peers—mostly from the Black Power faction— to take up violence as a form of self-defense. He wanted civil rights protest to be patient, intelligent and non-violent.

Back in Vietnam, I chuckled at the memory of the quick turnaround in thinking by the staff at the Neptune. And I felt ennobled by my memories of the Dr. King address. So, when I looked around now on the streets in Saigon, seeing black and white soldiers running in and out of the same places, eating in the same mess hall, sharing guard duty, or patrolling the streets—all as one, I knew this mingling was no accident.

Pioneers had cleared the forests of resistance to social equality on many fronts. Even my own schooling had been segregated until I was a senior in high school. As it were, I had a little hand in seeing things change at my alma mater. I sat back and gave it a thought. The momentum of social change in America came to Coats, at last, in the end of the fateful summer of 1965, for this was the time when our high school accepted its first black student in the history of the school.

Coats High School had been lily white since its inception in 1926. We had heard integration was coming for a few years, but it was still a shock to know the day of reckoning had actually arrived. In the local white community, only a few people like me, were pleased to see this day. Although we were nervous about it, most white people in the community were resigned, if not happy, about the forced changes underway. There was a minority of white people, however, who were mad as hell and were ready to strike back at the powers that be for letting their way of life change. The atmosphere at home was beginning to be crackling, just as it had been throughout the first half of 1965, as the ground forces for the civil rights movement began swarming throughout the South.

The civil rights news we were seeing on television and reading about in the papers was not a mirage; foremost among them the Selma civil rights march.

The first march began on March 7, when six hundred civil rights activists, including Hosea Williams of the SCLC and John Lewis of the Student Nonviolent Coordinating Committee (SNCC), left Selma, traveling eastward toward Montgomery, the state capitol. But on the first day they were met with violent resistance by state troopers and local police, who stopped the marchers at the Edmund Pettus Bridge, beating them with clubs as well as spraying them with water hoses and tear gas. Two days later, Martin Luther King led a march to the Pettus Bridge, but turned the marchers around at the bridge. On March 21, three thousand marchers left Selma for Montgomery, completing the march without opposition. On March 25, around twenty-five thousand people joined the Selma marchers at the Montgomery city limits.

Selma was a national awakening.

In Selma's aftermath, we were surprised, and some inspired, by President Lyndon Johnson's speech before a joint-session of Congress to advance the 1965 Voting Rights bill when he claimed for Selma a place among historic moments in the nation's history to be a free government when he said: "At times history and fate meet at a single time in a single place to shape a turning point in man's unending search for freedom. So it was at Lexington and Concord. So it was a century ago at Appomattox. So it was last week in Selma, Alabama.

"Rarely are we met with a challenge, not to our growth or abundance, or our welfare or our security, but rather to the values and purpose and the meaning of our beloved nation."

Doing more than mere talking, on August 6, President Johnson signed the Voting Rights Act into law, which outlawed such discriminatory voting requirements, like requiring a literacy test before registering to vote, that white Southerners had used to deprive black Southerners of the vote.

Thus, we knew the movement was winding its way to our own communities. As far as the idea of integrated public schools went, we were familiar with the eleven year old Brown vs. Board of Education decision by the U. S. Supreme Court that had declared segregation of public schools unlawful. We knew integration of the schools was only a matter of time, even for our little community. But, until now it had been a thought that was out-of-sight and out-of-mind.

The other threat, as far as white people were concerned, including Harnett County, and the whole of North Carolina, was that the peaceful forces for racial justice lead by Dr. King and the Southern Christian Leadership Conference, and the National Association for the Rights of Colored People (NAACP), would be supplanted by the violence-prone civil rights gangs. It was feared that these renegade groups would strike out at the white establishment; thus, increasing violence everywhere. After all, we had seen riots in the Watts section of Los Angeles in August, where roughly 34 blacks were killed, ignited by a charge of police brutality by a white cop against a local black man.

These kinds of social disturbances were galvanizing: white bigots were rising up to strike back; moderate whites were watching and waiting, and white progressives were taking more overt action on behalf of civil rights progress.

While the 1965 fall school term was set to begin in my hometown, we were bracing for what would come. The fast paced civil rights events of the year loomed in our minds. But it was our turn now.

With the Watts riots only weeks behind us, our nerves were on edge when the Coats High School opened its doors to the fall batch of new students, which included one black senior, a male named Ronald Womack. There were two black girls admitted to lower grades, as well. But all the attention was on the young man in the senior class of 1965-66.

I walked into the principal's office on that first day of school full of trepidation. There were rumors galore running around that said we'd see violence before the day was over. We heard that the new African American student was a NAACP plant, which somehow made him seem more dangerous. We heard there were white farmers waiting in parked cars nearby, shotguns ready. If these rumors weren't unnerving enough, the excited buzz of our own students in the hallways, many hostile, surly, and stressed, made the fear in the air tangible.

As far as I knew, as I mingled through the crowds greeting returning classmates, I would have no special role in the unfolding of events on this day. I was nervous, as much as anything, because I was the president of the student council, newly elected from the spring before, and I knew my first duty would be to make morning announcements over the intercom, a message that would go to all the classrooms. This was the customary duty of the student government president. I had eagerly campaigned to become president, but now had to do the actual work of the position. So, I made my way to the principal's office where the intercom was located.

I got there, pushing through the crowded doorway. Teachers were hurrying to their classrooms, other students were there because they had some particular need, and I believe one kid was already sick.

The principal's secretary gave me a batch of papers that had the messages I had to proclaim "on air." Then she showed me how to cut the machine on, and which dials to move to connect to certain classrooms. There were three areas to click on to: the high school rooms, the middle school rooms (as they would be called today) and the elementary rooms. Ours was a Union school, which meant our rambling school complex housed classes from first grade through the senior class. The building housing the high school grades was a huge two-story brick facility with high ceilings, large windows and gleaming, dark hard wood floors. There was no kindergarten provided at our school.

Principal J. C. Hawley greeted me and said he was looking forward to working with me. It was all friendly as we gathered around the intercom. It occurred to me we were ignoring the big elephant in the room, which was the fact we were letting in black students today. Nevertheless, I schmoozed with the principal some more until it was time to make the announcements, which we then commenced to do. Mr. Hawley made the introductory remarks, which were short and sweet. He announced that the high school grades would meet later for an assembly program. He then handed over to me the chore of going over other activities. I did it without error, to my great relief. Neither of us made mention of the fact that we would be having black students in our midst for the first time ever.

I was about ready to get to class when Mr. Hawley told me to hold up a minute. He said, "Come with me, Charles, I want to introduce you to our new student." "Sure," I said. He took me into the next room where I laid my eyes for the first time on our new black senior, Ronald Womack: here was our big elephant in the room, staring back at me, eyes wide with fear, sitting politely in the corner. He got up and extended his hand. I shook hands with him. It was an awkward and tentative moment. I didn't know what to do next.

"Well, Charles is our new student council president," Mr. Hawley said cheerfully, putting his hand on my shoulder. Then he turned to me and said quietly, "It's your job to show our new senior around. Here is his class schedule and his homeroom assignment. Go with him and get him oriented, okay?" He gave us a big grin, turned on his heels and walked back into his office, closing the door.

Me? I thought. *Oh, God,* why *me?* I felt a stab of
fear run through me. I shifted my eyes back to Ronald.
He looked scared, too. I also noticed that he had a
kind, lightly skinned, face. He was neatly dressed, not
a threatening kid, by any means. His congenial looks
would work in his favor, I felt. Ronald, having sat
back down, stayed glued to his seat. He wasn't eager
to leave the relative safety of the principal's office, any
more than me. He was quiet as a mouse.

"Hey, Ron," I said.

"Hey, Charles."

"You nervous?"

"Guess I am."

"Me, too."

We still stared at each other, both of us reluctant to
leave the safety of the principal's office.

"Ready?" I asked, moving to the door.

"Okay," he said, as he slowly got up.

"Well, we just need to act natural and get on with
it, I guess."

"Sure enough, Charles."

I didn't mistake Rod's bashful behavior to lack of
courage. He was simply figuring out how to perform,
how to not draw flak, and to fit in. He needed to find
a balance between being too submissive and too
assertive. I sensed he needed such a balance, too.
Every student, whites included, was challenged to
perform to some extent, to find a way to fit in, but not
to the extent that Ronald had.

We continued to stand there, still frozen in our fear, despite our small talk. A few more seconds dragged by and my fear somehow seemed to morph into a larger thought: this is not just a scary moment, this is a defining moment.

I had been talking the talk all my life, now I had a chance to walk the walk. Going on about human rights, being fair, and so on was fine for discussions, but this was for real. It all boiled down to how we would treat this kid in front of me.

I thought that Mr. Hawley was right, after all, it was my job to show him around and to get him started on the right track, just like any other new student. So, I patted Ronald on the shoulder and told him we needed to get going. I squared my shoulders to go, and then stopped. Another thought occurred to me, an epiphany really, that calmed me down considerably: *I am the right guy for this job.*

So, we walked out of the principal's office and rounded the corner to go down the long, narrow hallway, our objective being to get to the second floor where his classes were located. All I could hear was the thumping of our hearts and the click-clack of our shoes on the freshly varnished hardwood floor.

"Ron, hang tight with me," I said.

"You got it," he replied.

I look around and the strangest thing happened. The overflowing hallway began to part like the Red Sea as we walked down through its center. It was a sea of white faces, all pretty much awestruck, unsmiling, tense and oddly quiet. I glanced at Ronald; he was looking straight ahead, rigid. We went up the steps, still clearing the way, people stumbling back. One kid moved aside, while putting his finger to his nose, as if encountering a bad smell. We ignored him and kept on going. But nobody said anything or did anything to us. We made it safely.

I was sweating with relief. "Look, Ron, it's going to be tough, no way around it. But so far, so good."

"Yeah, it's all right," he said in a soft voice. He was very quiet and still nervous, but I sensed he was determined to see it through.

"Well, this is your home room and you have these numbers to get to where your classes are assigned." I checked his card that had the room numbers and the subjects he was taking. I explained where they all were. I felt the need to say a little more. "And, just to let you know, as you recall, I'm president of the student council. We'll be there for you, if there's trouble. Just let me know. Okay?"

"Thanks, Charles. I'll let you know," he said.

Yet, remarkably, he never once asked me or anybody else I know of, for any help after that first day. I would see Ronald often throughout our senior year, usually as we would pass each other while changing classes. We always exchanged greetings, but rarely talked much. I can't say we became pals, but I think he knew I was ready to help him, if needed. I regret that I didn't reach out more to be a friend. He was not hurt physically during that fateful year, but he must have been very lonely.

And so a new day had begun at our school. We had a black senior in our midst. The kids' initial negative reaction to Ron came as much from the need to conform as it was from any individual animosity they held for him. The new normal, in regard to Ronald's presence, seem to be one of letting things be. The walls had not fallen down, the water fountains still worked, the homework assignments were still being given out, and the bells were ringing at the appointed times. There were girls trying to make the cheerleading squad, guys trying to make the football team. We were busy breaking into the new school year. The hallways remained crowded and were never quiet again like that first day. We had no time, really, to spend on hating this new guy. I wish I could say the same for a few folks outside the school.

By lunch time my mother got a call from the head of the local bank. He told her he'd heard I had become buddies with the new black kid. We were a pair, he'd been told, and this was going to go bad for me. He heard a bunch of boys were planning to beat me up at the local football game to be played on the upcoming Friday night.

Well, my mother was rightfully alarmed by this news. And one never wanted to get on the bad side of Mildred. She arranged for my brother, Johnny, and a few of his friends to follow me around to make sure no harm came to me.

I didn't know I was in any danger. As far as I was concerned, it had been a great week. The football game would top off a successful first week of school. I was happy that there'd been no violence at school because of Ronald. Since the tension of the first day, everybody was more or less back to normal.

There had been a few instances of students being rude, even crude, to Ronald, but nothing physical had happened. He was a model student for the situation he was in. Later on, I heard that he was half-German. His father was a black American soldier and his mother a German. They met while his father was stationed in Germany shortly after World War II. Our maid, Nellie, knew about it and said Ronald had been sent to America because "they didn't want him." So, Ron had already known worse rejection than his classmates could dispense to him. He could not be drawn out by anything bad said to him, or by any taunts. After a while, it got old messing with him, so he was left alone. And that was enough for me.

So, as things turned out, I went to the football game, had a nice time and came home none the wiser of my danger. The alleged plot to get me may have been fabricated, who knows? It was great to know Johnny and company had my back that evening.

It was a relief, but no accident, that Coats had had no violence at the beginning of its school year in 1965.

There had been sporadic violence at other North Carolina public schools desegregating at this time, but not in our town. Around my home town, I felt the whites and blacks had been in close proximity for a long time, had worked together in the tobacco and cotton fields, had exchanged greetings on Saturday shopping days, and so on, for so long that it had made our races too familiar with each other to build up the resentment needed to cause violence.

How do people kindle the fire to club, hit or shoot each other when they know each other's names, and the names of each other's children? If I needed to prove my point, I only had to look to Chicago and Boston to see how violent their desegregation efforts were, largely because the battling whites and blacks saw each other as only alien groups, not as friends or neighbors they knew anything about.

The fall of 1965 saw many public schools in North Carolina finally integrate for the first time since the law prohibiting segregation in public schools had been enacted 11 years earlier in the Brown v. Board of Education case. The new spurt of activity was brought about by recent federal court decisions that enacted guidelines to actively integrate the public schools. In short, the courts were saying it was no longer acceptable for integration to exist in theory alone; it was time to implement the law to make it happen. "With all deliberate speed" would no longer emphasize "deliberate" over "speed," it seemed.

In the case of a minority trying to assimilate into the majority, the absence of violence alone was not ultimately fulfilling. In the case of Ronald Womack in our school, his victory would have been incomplete if his daily existence had been nothing but persistent isolation, where he felt he was never a real part of our senior class. While this brave young man, on the whole, had to feel set apart from his white classmates, there were some breakthroughs I hoped let him know he was recognized as our peer, at least, by many of us.

One breakthrough for Ronald came by an act of kindness shown to him by an unlikely fellow senior. This small miracle happened around Christmas 1965. We seniors were gathering outside to have a group photo taken. The photographer was positioning us to pose in a wide semi-circle, so we were milling around to get in our right places. We boys had been told to wear neckties, for some reason, and we were all so adorned except for Ronald, who upon discovering his error, began to back away. He told us to go ahead with the photo session without him. Well, some hesitation set in, we looked back and forth, and it looked like Ronald was going to walk away.

It didn't happen. One of our seniors, a gregarious guy named Joe Byrd, suddenly grabbed Ronald by the shoulder, turned him around, and had him stand next to him in our evolving semi-circle.

"You're a senior, too. Just stay next to me."

He glanced around, almost as if to dare anyone to

disagree with him. Nobody objected, and we all turned our attention to striking our pose for the photographer, who never brought up the requirement that the boys needed a necktie.

The 1966 high school annual includes this photo of us in the outside semi-circle. It's a nice photo. We are all there, smiling, side-by-side. Joe is there, next to Ronald, and the rest of us are there in an orderly fashion. Since the photo was taken from a distance, the fact that one lone senior boy is minus a necktie is unnoticeable. But it is noticeable that we had an integrated class. Our originality, in that regard, is chronicled, with Ronald's smiling face intertwined with the rest of us. I'd say to Joe, as the British do,

"Well done."

12

Mostly, our troops behaved well as guests in a foreign country. I was proud of my compatriots, over all. However, being far from home, sadly, also brought out the worst in some. A bad guy is going to be a bad guy, no matter if he is wearing a tuxedo, a three-piece suit or a decorated uniform. For example, I should have hated all Navy seamen because on my first night at the hotel in Saigon, the guy whose room I was taking over—he was going home to America that day— suckered me into paying him $15 dollars for a lamp and clock that he said he was leaving behind. Good, but when I returned that evening from work, he was gone, the lamp and clock were gone, and so was my $15 dollars. And he was a white Southerner!

One day we had a staff meeting presided over by CSM Wilson. He told us that we all had to cough up about $15 dollars for a detachment holiday party. It was to be a big six-course meal catered by a fine Chinese restaurant. Entertainment would be provided, he added with a grin. Strippers, actually. We were reluctant to contribute because fifteen dollars was a pretty hefty amount. But the peer pressure was on to pony up. One guy tried to hold out, but Wilson needed about thirty seconds to impress on him that it would be in his best interests to fork over his due.

So, we all showed up for the fine dinner, even taking our Vietnamese office staff. I invited one of our section secretaries, a shy Vietnam woman named Lien, unlike some of the guys who brought girls they had picked up in bars. I was careful, as I always was, to make our evening out an extension of our office relationship, not a social outing. We met at the party and parted at the party. I had some occasions to have legitimate Vietnamese girls show me attention, but I knew it would be a tragedy to lead them on. Most all the Vietnamese women we knew wanted to go to America, and if it took marrying an American to get there—and that was by far the best method—so be it. I knew this kind of hook up could lead to disaster down the road. I didn't want to lead any of these disparate girls on, as many soldiers did. It wasn't that I was a saint, but it simply wasn't necessary to get a girl in bed by promising to marry her and bring her to America.

There were plenty of girls to be had if one was willing to pay the price, literally and otherwise.

Yet, I did let my guard down one time with a "straight" Vietnamese girl, a secretary who'd invited me and a couple of other guys to her house to celebrate her birthday. We thought, *why not?*

We took a taxi to her neighborhood and paid our fare, then set to walking down the street—or path to be more accurate—to the address she had given us. It was getting dark, for one thing, and we were inundated by the clamor of the closely packed Vietnamese neighbors, the smells of open cooking emitting God knows what. The settlement was a conglomeration of plywood, corrugated metal, and sheets of plastic and cardboard boxes, not to mention wastewater puddles scattered about. The sewer stink and rotten fish smell had us holding our noses part of the way. We had the scary feeling of being on the dark side of the moon. But we pushed on until we entered upon some better looking houses, less cluttered, and there were even some assorted strands of colored lights—red, blue, green, etc.—adding a little carnival atmosphere, despite the otherwise bleak environs. But I knew the lights were obscuring many suspicious faces, so we kept moving. But as we walked on, I instructed the other two guys to mind their manners when we got there. I was worried how they would act in front of the girl's parents, both elderly, who would be hosting the party.

"Look, you guys eat whatever it is they set before

us, okay?" I said.

"Sure, Charlie, but I hope I don't get sick," said Jimmy, who worked in accounting.

"Don't make faces, either, if you can help it," I said, still worried.

"We'll be all right, Charlie, relax," Jimmy said.

"Well, I had to calm you guys down last week when you wouldn't shut up at that Buddhist temple. People were praying in there," I said.

"Ah, shit, man, we were getting high off that incense."

"Yeah, right. I can't take you people anywhere."

"Speaking of anywhere, Charlie, where the hell are we going now?"

"We're almost there," I said as I examined the numbers on the shacks we were passing.

"I hope we make it out of here alive," Scott, the other soldier said, his eyes wide open in fear.

About that time, we encountered a group of about six rough looking Vietnamese toughs, or "cowboys," as they were called. They gave us a fierce look, but passed on by. We all breathed a sigh of relief.

We finally found her little house—a tiny place with a corrugated roof and screened in front porch. The birthday girl, Louise, as I recall, was beautifully dressed in a native gown, ankle length and in black and brown colors, topped off by having a white flower in her hair. She met us at the door, smiled warmly and bowed slightly and stepped aside to let us come inside.

We stopped for an instant at the front door, surprised by the chicken coops on each side, both with live chickens in them. But once we got inside, the small room was richly adorned. There was some fine looking furniture of deeply carved wood. Her parents, who had held back at first, were dignified and bowed to us like we were royalty. We wound up having a delightful meal, served in at least four courses, always with white rice, noodles, spices and beef and chicken. We were not always sure of what we were eating, but it was good. The aroma was to die for. I did suffer drinking the hot beer, but I smiled when I took a sip and glared at my buddies to do the same. Jimmy looked pale when he swallowed his beer, but he held his cool. At long last, we left the party and thanked the little family for their kindness. We darted down the path, parting the boisterous, curious crowd, so we could get back to safe ground. We didn't tell our superiors about our outing; we knew Army regulations discouraged GIs from fraternizing with the Vietnamese civilians in their living territories. In the slums we had gone to, I hate to think of how many Viet Cong were living there. We were lucky to not have been jumped.

A few days later Louise called me on the phone and told me how much she enjoyed our visit. She said her parents approved of us, as well. She wanted to meet again. She was innocent, but I knew if I set up anymore visits, especially for just us, I would be leading her on, and that would be crossing the line, officially and ethically, as far I was concerned. Still, she was a sweet girl and distancing me from her was hard to do.

Later, I would see miserable Vietnamese brides in Fayetteville, N. C. with their American husbands who were based at nearby Fort Bragg. There were so many divorces after the war that Fayetteville had a section entitled "Little Saigon," and it was filled with jilted Vietnamese ex-wives, many now sadly back in the bar girl business. Yet, most American soldiers felt if a Vietnamese woman hustled us and begged us for companionship, etc., then we were not corrupting her to take her up on her proposition. Some of us stayed clear of prostitutes and bar girls on practical grounds because getting hooked on this activity was froth with danger. Many of the girls had bandit boyfriends that would move in and rob the soldier, literally with his pants down in the hotel room.

Our crime blotters were filled nightly with armed robbery and assault cases, mostly by South Vietnamese soldiers, or South Vietnamese civilians, against our servicemen. Most of these incidents were because our guys—black and white-- were in the wrong place at the wrong time—and that added up to being drunk in a bar or hotel somewhere. It was bad business, all in all. One guy in our detachment, a corporal from Alabama named Ray, lost a pile of money when he let a bar girl, who had been waiting for him nightly at a Du Do Street tavern talk him into paying the down payment on the monthly rent for an apartment they were to share. She had fooled him by wearing traditional Vietnamese dress and was lovey-dovey in the most innocent way, causing him to think she cared for him more than his money. He gave her the money, at long last, and she, in turn, gave him the address of the apartment. She told him to wait until the next night to meet her there. He put it this way to me, while crying in his beer, at a soldier beer hall near our billet.

"Charlie, damn, I got the address and took a taxi to the address. Shit, man, it was a narrow path, almost, wall-to-wall shacks," he said.

"Really?" I said. "Were you suspicious off the bat?"

"Sort of, but, you know, love is blind," he said, his eyes downcast. He played around with his beer mug. Then he blinked hard and went on.

"Yeah, I asked a mama son about the address. She got a couple of other locals to examine my piece of paper with the address on it. They were chattering real good, really excited."

"That doesn't sound good, Ray."

"Naw, and it won't. Mama son pointed out the place that was supposed to be our apartment, and it was a little shoe shop or something there. Not a goddam apartment, that's for sure."

"What'd you do then?" I asked. I felt for him now, but I also thought he'd been really naïve.

"Well, shit, I could see I'd been had. I walked off."

"How you seen her since?"

"Naw, I went back to the bar for three or four nights, but she was long gone. None of them gooks knew where she'd gone, either. If they knew, they won't going to tell me."

"Ray, you've learned a lesson the hard way. But at least you've got your life. It's best to stick to buying a Saigon Tea, my friend," I said.

"You got that right," Ray said. "At least I didn't get worked over by one of her cowboys."

"True, Ray. I see the MP blotter every day and plenty of our guys are kicking their ass kicked by the cowboys, city thugs, or whatever we call them."

"And they're supposed to be on our side? What the fuck!" he said.

"As I said, Ray, live and learn."

"I will, Charlie. Thanks," he said. Then he looked at me directly, his eyes watering, his face a mirror of regret. "I just wanted a girl, that's all. I never had a girl. Look at me. I'm no catch."

He wiped his tears away with his beefy hand.

"Don't you say nothing, okay, Charlie?"

"I won't, buddy. My lips are sealed."

"Yeah. Ain't asking for much, is it? Damn, this girl, wow, she just seemed so sweet, so real. She wasn't no slut. She was dressed traditional, you know, the long dress, and her hair up in a bun."

"I know, she wasn't a party girl type, for sure."

"Yeah, I just wanted a girl. When I get home, I'll be a loser again. Here, I'm Number One, you know. Ha, what a joke."

At that point, we shook hands and Ray sadly walked off to get to bed early. He said he was done with bar hopping. I worried about Ray and looked in on him fairly often, but he seemed to get over it, at least, on the outside. His story was one of thousands of lonely GIs getting fleeced or worse on by seducers in the red light sections of Saigon.

A really sad case I learned about involved an American soldier and his Vietnamese girlfriend, both found dead in the apartment he was renting off base. They were found naked and lying on their bed. It turned out he had promised to marry her and bring her back to America. That promise had kept her in a state of bliss for many months, friends said, but when his departure date drew near, he told her he was not going to marry her. He told her he was leaving without her. His attitude was callus and stupid. He didn't factor in, while forming his shameless exit plan, that his girlfriend's religious belief held that if they died together on earth, they would live together forever in heaven. She shot him in the head with his own gun before she turned the gun on herself. Our office, it was told to me, authored a letter explaining that this cad had been killed by an "enemy female Communist agent." What good would it do to tell his parents the truth? I thought this was the compassionate thing to do, as well. This bedroom killing was another chilling reason to tread carefully.

Regrettably, some of our dangers in Saigon were of our own making. My most foolish experience, I suppose, was when I kept drinking mixed drinks one evening—which were being secretly spiked by my fellow MPs--at yet another of our detachment parties. I was not used to mixed drinks, growing up in a dry county in North Carolina, so I was merrily going along, drinking away and wondering why my glass seemed to stay full. As the evening wore on and our detachment party began to wane, three of us piled into a cab to go to a local lounge to hear a little music and mess around with whoever might show up there— meaning girls. It was a high end, frenchified Vietnamese place. We were all in the lobby, as best I can recall, sitting around talking. I believe one guy paired off with a woman, leaving me to hang out with the remaining guy. It was getting dull.

And that is all I remember until I woke up lying on the ceramic floor of a bathroom up a few floors. About an hour had passed since I'd been downstairs. I slowly awoke, feeling groggy as I've ever felt. I looked up at a door and then a mirror. Suddenly, I realized where I was and felt a stab of fear. I reached for my wallet. *God, it's still on me!* I thought. I was surprised that I had not been rolled. I got up, braced myself against the wall to get my bearings. I had a buzz on, but it was dissipating rapidly. I became stone sober when I looked at my watch and realized it was passed the dreadful curfew when we were supposed to be in our billet and off the streets. Yet, here I was in civilian clothes, a rare condition, and, worse, several blocks away from our billet. This was not good. *And where were my so called friends? Damn them*, I thought. *How could they leave me, if I'd passed out?*

I splashed some cold water on my face from the bathroom sink. I felt wide awake and cold sober now. I quickly got down the stairs and went out the side exit of the hotel. It was about 2 o'clock in the morning. At this hour, it could be assumed anybody I may meet would be trouble. As a foreigner in civilian clothes, I was suspect, as well. Actually, since I was not armed, I was like a lamb strolling around for the slaughter. I leaned against the wall in the alley and decided I had no choice but to meander back on the sly.

I dared not take the main thoroughfare, which would have been my choice to get to our billet in the daylight hours. So, I scampered and weaved myself through about a mile of back alleys. Every time I heard a sound, I'd duck behind a bush or parked truck or whatever. At one point, I accidentally kicked a metal saucer and stirred a small flock of chickens in a small coop attached to a Vietnamese lean-to house. A dog barked, as well. I froze and let the clatter die down. I thought I saw somebody move a curtain, but I knew they couldn't see me in the shadows. After a safe interval, I went on.

Finally, after about forty-five minutes, I sneaked up to the fire escape in the rear of our hotel. I could see the two guard huts up front and knew they were being manned. I figured the guards were too trigger-happy to risk hailing them to let me in. Also, there was the risk I could get turned in, even if the guards didn't shoot me. So, I got a box and stood on it to give me enough height to grab the bottom of the fire escape. I pulled myself up on it, never making a sound. I then climbed up until I got to my floor, on the fourth level. I turned the doorknob, figuring it was going to be locked, but to my amazement, the door opened. "Jesus," I muttered. *I must be living right*, I thought. I continued to sneak down the hall and quietly entered my room. My roommate was in bed, probably drunk, and snoring loud enough to peel the ceramic down the walls. I made it back safety, after all. I reported for duty right on time the next morning at 7 a.m. I had some sharp comments to make to my so called friends, to say the least.

The other foolish thing I did was to "borrow" our detachment van for "unauthorized" use one evening. We had heard there was a great new movie out called *Mash*, and since we'd heard it trashed the military, we had to see it. It never occurred to us that the oppressive military was allowing us to see the irreverent film. We just knew then that this was a film not to miss.

Since I was the courier for our detachment, I had the keys to the van. We plotted that evening about how to get to Ton Son Nhut Air Force Base, where the theater was located, so we could see the movie and get back without detection. Basically, we knew we'd be okay if we didn't get into an accident on the road, or God forbid, actually get shot at by the enemy. I figured that was not likely, so all five of us piled in and I drove the group to Ton Son Nhut.

Nothing like draftees watching a movie showing the hypocrisies of the military world we felt we'd been abducted into. Yet, looking around at the audience, I saw all grades of officers and lifers in the crowd, all laughing their butts off. Again, I was reminded in a tangible way that the guys and gals in the military were more than a sum of their parts. These folks were laughing at the same stuff that I was laughing at, all the while doing their jobs for the system under attack by the movie. They might be bound to the military, but they were not its clones. *It is not them against me*, I thought. *It's not that simple.*

We all piled out of the movie, juiced up by the parody on men at war. I made it home safely, even though we had a few near misses with a few taxi drivers and cyclo operators. And we barely missed a cow strolling along the middle of the road. So, I checked off my second foolish outing.

Saigon was unpredictable. There were no front lines or rear lines in an exact sense. One evening I had been out to see a friend at another post and took a cyclo home. It was not terribly late and I wasn't worried about the curfew. The Vietnamese driver delivered me near to my billet, and I got out to pay him. I realized I didn't have enough money to pay the exorbitant price he expected from an American. I tried to explain my plight and told him, as best I could, that the fair market price would have to do. I gave him the money, shrugged, and attempted to step away. The driver was a tough, leathery, old guy about fifty. He gave me a bad look; he was not buying it. As I tried to walk off the curb, he shifted in front of me, demanding more money. Then, I turned to my left, and he blocked me; I turned to my right, and he blocked me again.

"I've have no more money!" I said.

"Need more!" he said. He waved the batch of piasters I'd given him in disgust.

I had had enough. I shoved him to the side and walked straight forward, hoping to leave him standing there with the correct fare he would expect from any Vietnamese.

I never saw it coming.

He silently sneaked up from behind and coldcocked me, landing his fist to the side of my head. The pain pushed through my left ear against my skull. I fell forward and landed on my knees. My head was hanging down. My spectacles were shattered on the ground. I raised my head, looked around, but without my glasses, could see nothing but a mix of dark and light, blending together like a kaleidoscope. Then I came up on one knee, stood up and turned around. Flushed with anger, I charged at him. My head was on fire, mostly from the ringing in my ear. I wanted to hammer this little piss ant.

But I could barely see him as he ran down a dark alley. I followed him for a few more steps before my brain began to kick in. I knew if I followed him down that alley, it would turn out badly for me. If there was a fight, the bystanders, certainly Vietnamese, would join in—not to help an American— but to help this fellow beat the hell out of me, or worse. It was called "cluster" fighting. So, I stopped in my tracks. I turned around, scooped up the remnants of my glasses, and walked briskly back to my billet. I shrugged it off, figuring it could have been worse, compared to senseless shootings, knifings and bombings that popped up in Saigon, much less the vicious violence in the jungles. Nevertheless, I was blind as a bat for about three days until I got new glasses. And I made sure to get a backup pair, as well.

13

As if getting knocked in the head wasn't bad enough, I ran into another close call in downtown Saigon a few weeks later, when I had a close call with a few whizzing bullets.

I was going to drop into a bar for a quick beer before returning to my billet, when I stopped in my tracks on the sidewalk about 100 feet from the entrance. I saw a couple of soldiers run and rush my way. I just stood there as they went by me. Boy, they looked scared, I thought. And for good reason. In a second a little Vietnamese guy came out, a civilian I reckoned by his dandy looking clothes. But he was brandishing a small pistol and he looked angry. He took aim at the two soldiers that has just passed me and opened fire. I luckily was standing near a telephone pole and ducked behind it. I sucked my stomach in and just froze right there. Several bullets rang by, really close. After the guy emptied the gun—about five rounds—he stomped back into the bar. I peeked out and saw that the action was over. The sidewalk quickly became crowded again. Gunfire was not unusual in this wild west of a place. But I lost my appetite for anything to drink and caught a rickshaw back to my billet.

I didn't feel like going straight to bed, so I walked up the stairs to the roof of our building. During the day the mama sons hung laundry on clothes lines there, but at night it was quiet and dark, far above the din of the busy, bright and loud street life of the city. It was literally an "Up on a Roof" place for me. I leaned against the outer wall and gazed at the moon with its soft yellow glow and at the galaxy of white twinkling stars, the same view I knew the people at home were looking at— always a comforting thought. I knew I was lucky to be in Saigon, but I had to be more careful about rambling around on the streets at night. I needed to avoid trouble, not go looking for it.

My dad had to avoid dangers when he was in the service, too. I knew he'd gotten out of his share of scrapes overseas in the Pacific, as well when he was in training at Notre Dame, Northwestern and in San Francisco. His troubles didn't end when he was discharged, either. I wondered if I would share his fate. I felt at peace thinking of home, nevertheless.

My dad's World War II letters were full of agony about missing home. He thought the world would be only right if he could get back to my mother. Boy was he wrong. Yet, my dad really tried to make things work, either in the Navy or at home. His example always made me want to hang in there, too. I still thought of him every day, even though he had been dead for over ten years. I thought of him mainly when I was alone and not distracted. I settled in and began to think of him pretty hard in my little hide away "Up on the Roof."

My father was among massive numbers of veterans were returning home following the end of World War II, so decent jobs were scarce due to the increased competition. There were more men home now than there were jobs. My dad initially returned to the farm. He tried that for a while, and found he wasn't much good at it. He had grown up on a farm, and maybe that was the problem. He knew how oppressive farm life could be. His dad had endured a lifetime as a tobacco farmer in eastern North Carolina. My dad was one of five boys, and all of them abandoned the family farm for greener pastures. My father had moved to Harnett County specifically to start up a Motorola dealership, selling televisions and other electrical products, all part of a four store chain. He later added a number of small business enterprises—shoe shop, café, beauty parlor, plumbing and heating and a gas station—to have a cash flow to augment the key dealership whose activities where not under his sole control. He pretty quickly had a little empire going on and his businesses extended for a whole block on Main Street in Coats. We'd go in one store and then to the next; they were all ours. Aside from renting the several store spaces, he also had the responsibility for paying for loads of material, supplies, trucks and equipment, not mention a sizable payroll. He was spreading himself thin to make his multi-faceted operations turn a profit. He was generating a lot of gross revenue, but his problem was that his overhead costs were more than keeping pace with his net profits.

My father lost the businesses in just a few years. He wrote in a letter I found that that the business he had direct control over was profitable, but his partners' losses in their stores was what took them all down. Apparently, he was part of a small franchise arrangement where the expenses and profits were pooled, so it was possible that the weak link was not him, and, thus, the failure was not his fault alone. But my mother always placed the blame squarely on my dad's shoulders. She thought his whole idea of trying to investing in a small, rural town like Coats was nothing more than a pig in a poke. She faulted him for being too trusting and allowing customers to not pay what they owed him. And we heard stories, mostly from her, about him being better at promoting than at collecting. He, in all probability, extended too much credit, purchased too many supplies, and let his compassion overtake his prudence.

One story I heard was that Uncle Boots, who worked for a while in our family business, sold several bicycles to boys around town, all for only a verbal promise to make payments. None of them were heard from again. The thing about this failure that would forever haunt him was that he had gotten substantial financial backing from friends and family, and the family money was from my mother's side. She would forevermore bring up the loss of "her" money to him, when it suited her. Most of her family money had come when she and her widowed mother, Nanny, sold the farm, which precipitated the move from her home county in eastern North Carolina to Harnett County.

If my father had defaulted on his obligations to a bank, it would have been only a financial failure, but by losing the money of his friends and family, it became a moral failure in his mind. I believe this rock bottom outcome made him turn all his energies to settling things up. And he set out to do just that, to the extent that he rarely could relax, or laugh, or take a deep breath, ever again. After my father's unprofitable experience running a business with partners, and then finding that public work didn't pay enough, he tried direct sales to make ends meet. He had a gift for gab, always a good foundation for the sales world, if there were paying customers to be found. Always a big "if."

But it was not to be.

One short-lived sales effort by my father was to sell vacuum cleaners. He went to a home on appointment and was trying his best to demonstrate his wares. He had a little device on the machine to do gentle things, like drapes, so he applied the device to the curtains he saw hanging nearby. The problem was they were paper curtains. The vacuum sucked them off the rods, shredding them. He had to pay for the damages. Suffice to say, he did not make the sale. This was one example of his hard luck.

He also labored to sell Compton encyclopedias. We had a set at home, which he probably purchased, but I'm not sure many other families in Harnett County had any. To add insult to injury, one evening my mother took an appointment for him, when he couldn't make it, to show the encyclopedias. She went out there and sold a set on her only attempt. When she kidded him about it afterwards, he would shrug his shoulders, drag deeply on his cigarette, and say she only made the sell because they wanted to get her out of the house to shut her up. I loved it when they bantered like this.

And so it was that my father labored throughout the 1950s: not getting ahead, not falling behind either. To his credit, he kept a roof over our heads, clothes on our backs, and food on our table. We had the basics, but little more.

We were able to go to Atlantic Beach sometimes,

and there was a trip to the Blue Ridge Mountains, but our mainstays were our frequent trips to my father's family home in Martin County, especially during the Christmas holidays. My dad's favorite thing to do was visit his home. He had four brothers and two sisters, who he drew strength from and with whom he could share his troubles without fear of being harshly judged.

My dad especially loved to sit up late with his closest sister, Ruby, and talk, drink coffee and smoke cigarettes late into the night at the kitchen table. They were kindred spirits, who came away buoyed from their time together. I used to love and sit at my uncle's knees and listen to their tall tales and country yarns. I had Boots, Tim, Wilmer, Pete, and Leon to choose from. Often they would sit on the front porch in the evening, in the dark except for the flares of their lighted cigarettes. My aunts would be in the lighted living room talking a mile a minute. Looking around at my aunts, I had Ruby, Keathley, Marie, Alice, Iva and Bessie to choose from. My cousins were Mike, Patti, Janice, Phillip and Eddie. We kids would run back and forth from each group, feeling like we were in a sort of folksy, loving incubator. We slept under several layers of quilted blankets on ice cold sheets in the ice cold room. In the mornings we ran to the kitchen, warmed by the fiery wood stove there, and satisfied our hunger by way of Aunt Bessie's eggs, bacon, grits and coffee, whose succulent aroma filling the air.

My aunts and uncles also loved to gather around,

sometimes outside by a barrel fire, to sing hymns and old ballads. They would say, "Let's harmonize." The rare times when my father would break into song was when we were driving to see his family.

While we witnessed my father's often morose demeanor as he constantly drove himself to make ends meet, we also saw our mother show the strain of getting by with her erratic moods and occasional temper tantrums. She was spoiled and could be fussy about the smallest of things. My dad ignored her complaints, for the most part, and so she would often direct her frustration our way. As children, we simply were scared or plain tired of her grumpiness, or crying spats. But she could also be charming and loving and full of enthusiasm. I was always amazed at how she could be standing there in the kitchen doing the dishes or cooking, and have this sing-song sort of whining going on, only to have the phone ring and immediately snap her out of her sorrow and become engaged in a happy conversation with who ever had called.

My mother also had the redeeming quality of never embarrassing us when we were in public. She always wanted to put a good face on. In fact, we knew that she had our back, no matter how petulant she could be. Our dad had schooled us to know she was spoiled, not hateful. One day, she proved her mettle with me. It went down this way:

We were all at a movie theater, enjoying a show, when my nose started bleeding. I was embarrassed, but couldn't just sit there bleeding all over everybody, so I rushed to the boy's bathroom. I was leaning over the basin, trying to stop the flow without much success. I was in a bad way. It was like somebody was dumping a jar of chunky salsa down the drain. Word of my plight got to my mother; however, and she had no qualms about bursting through the door to help me, boy's bathroom or not. She held me, while barking out orders to get wet cloths. She later laid me out on the theater manager's desk, until the bleeding stopped. I'm sure the head guy there was chagrined over that intrusion into his office, but I am sure, as well, that my mother gave him no choice. I've never known what brought on the giant nose bleed. What I will always take with me from that awful experience is the memory of her fierce actions to make sure I was all right.

By the next morning, after my calamity at the theater, she may well have been bitching about how nobody loved her and how the house was a mess, but that was the way it was. We never knew if things would run hot or cold or just right. She was a paradox, for sure. It could be maddening. Yet, she was the one who was there to lift us up and to pull things together, while our dad, as kind as he was, was the remote one.

As I said, my mother was usually the bad cop at home, while Dad would be the good guy. But he would intervene occasionally, and when he did, we were scared aplenty. He would use his belt, if need be, and he also had a whacking board he called the "Board of Education." That thing hurt. He never abused us, for it only took a few solid blows to get the message home.

I suppose the one whipping I got was one I truly deserved, and it came about when I let my desire to buy a little whistle I had seen at the McKnight drugstore in Coats cause me to lose all my good sense. I saw the whistle and really wanted it, but I didn't have any money. So, I went across the street and tried to get the bank to loan me a quarter. I was turned down by our sly bank manager, who I believed called my mother to let her know of my outlandish behavior. I was around nine or ten years old, at this time. To make matters worse, I went store-to-store: the Five and Dime, Lee's Clothing Store, and Earl's Grocery seeking the elusive quarter. The proprietors had the money, I'm sure, but in this display of a village raising a child, they each turned me down because they felt it was unseemly of a child with some means of support at home to be out and about publicly begging for money. I was disheartened at long last and sauntered home, feeling very annoyed.

But little did I know the trouble I was in. My mother apparently told my dad, or, worse, he may have heard about my expedition from one of the business people I had tried to get money from. He blew his stack! He was mortified that his son had gone out and begged for money. And to the bank, of all places! I walked into a buzz saw. I never saw my quiet dad so angry, really fussing at me. I cried and did all I could to say I was sorry, but it did no good. He pulled me across the dryer and whipped my butt, and it was done fairly well, too. For a change, my mother was the quiet one. To make matters worse, he sat with me at the kitchen counter and made me write down each name of where I had gone to borrow the money. He wrote out a legal sounding statement under my name expressing my apologies and had a place for the business proprietors to sign it. He said I had to get up the next morning and go to the businesses, apologize, and get the signatures. It was probably what I need to do, but I was too mortified by this time to have any rational thoughts on the matter.

Surprisingly, my mother stepped in to save me. Maybe, it was her pride that convinced her to intervene. She probably didn't like the idea of her son having to go around with his head down, seeking forgiveness. She convinced my father to let the corporal punishment be enough. So, when I got up the next morning and was beginning to slink out the door, the statement in my hand, and feeling lower than a snake, she came into the kitchen, gave me a hug, and said Dad had changed his mind and that I didn't have to get the paper signed. Whoa! I felt like the heavens had opened up and saved me from hell. And for that moment, Mom was my guardian angel.

14

As I continued to muse about my family back home, especially my dad, I could hear distant bombing and see the faraway flashes of the explosions in the night sky. But the booms were in the outlying areas, not in Saigon proper. Saigon had its share of bombings, but they were more likely to be hand grenades or sticks of dynamite thrown by Cong agents, either planted or thrown from a moving vehicle. Ours was urban fighting, apt to turn up anywhere and at any time. Regardless, Saigon was rightfully seen as a rearguard, safe haven in comparison to the horrors of the jungle, a.k.a. the "boonies." Few of we Saigon based soldiers would disagree with the notion that we had been dealt the better hand. But we still had to be careful. I got to the point, when I was walking the street or on currier duty in my van, that I could tell if a Vietnamese was hostile or not to me. I could see it in their eyes—dull and flat--even if they were smiling. Occasionally, if I found myself somewhere in downtown Saigon totally surrounded by Vietnamese, maybe in a market, or some shanty I had stopped by to look at a product, I got a cold feeling in my stomach that I was in the wrong place and made it my business to get back on the beaten path. The surface safety of the crowded city life, where we were rubbing elbows with Vietnamese of all types, constantly threw us off and gave us a false sense of security. I used to say it was akin to a Catholic or Protestant wandering into the wrong place in Belfast, Northern Ireland, where, before you knew it, one could be in alien territory, sometimes, to that wander's sorrow. My brother John often told me to "always be alert to my surroundings," and his lesson served me well for the most part.

Many soldiers wandered about unwisely in Saigon because they were sick of staying in close quarters with their buddies. They might be quartered in large, sprawling tent cities near MACV, or in civilian quarters, like our old, rundown hotel. The streets beckoned and our young spirits had to roam. We were lonesome, really, and moving around, risky as it might be, was better than being cooped up. I probably could have benefited from talking to a chaplain during those hot days and hot nights in Saigon, but I had lost my faith in them, if not in God, since I'd heard an Army clergyman gives a pro-war sermon while we were gathered in the woods on an icy cold Georgia morning when I was training at Fort Gordon. *How does he know God's plan for us*? I thought at the time. I wanted to question him, but we were busy gathering our gear to move out into the forest. But on the spot I built up a prejudice against chaplains, relegating them in my mind to nothing more than spiritual mercenaries. Even Abraham Lincoln, while in the midst his struggles in the American Civil War made the point in his writings that God's purposes are not directly knowable to humans. I felt Lincoln, as well, was writing directly to the defenders of the Vietnam War, including that cock-sure chaplain, when he penned these words: "Men are not flattered by being shown that there has been a difference of purpose between the Almighty and them."

I still think I had this guy pegged right, but my reaction to his message was as unbending as his message for us to do or die. I was wrong to blame all the military clergy for the one belligerent I had heard. I never went to a service while in Vietnam out of yet another act of conscience, as I saw it. I was content to pray directly to Jesus when I felt the need. What with my exposure to the Baptist belief in the "priesthood of all believers," I felt I was on solid ground.

I continued to listen to the night sounds from my perch atop our billet, and my thoughts drifted back again to my dad, who while aware of his surroundings, seemed to always struggle to gain control over them. Before the Wrightsville Beach opportunity came along, and just after a few years in direct sales, in the mid-1950s my father finally found professional, if not financial, stability as a probation officer, where he was assigned to cover Harnett, Johnston, Lee and Cumberland counties.

He was good at the probation job because his gift of empathy enabled him to be an effective counselor to people in trouble. I remember some of the probationers coming to our house in the evening. My father would sit and talk to them and urge them on. He would patiently listen to their problems, and excuses. They felt moved by his sincerity. While many of them came into our house feeling frustrated and guilt-ridden, following a session with my father, they would leave full of hope for better days.

But fate intervened one time in a tragic way for one young couple seeking my dad's help. On this occasion, this couple came and had the usual heart-to-heart talk with him. The husband was the one in trouble and seeking to rebuild his life and save his marriage. His wife was holding on to him, equally in earnest as him, to find their way on what they hoped would be a journey of renewal for them both. I was hearing parts of this exchange because I was hiding at the top of the stairs, just outside the bedroom I shared with Johnny. I think he was asleep. I was too much of a curiosity cat to miss any adult conversation that I had been told to stay away from. I heard my dad gave them advice and encouragement, sort of droning on, like he did when talking to me or my brothers. But these folks were all ears. After an hour or so, they thanked Dad, both giving him a hug, and left.

Within an hour, my father got a call telling him that this young man and woman had both been killed in a traffic accident on their way home. My father was as grief stricken over their death as he had been over his own brother's death. He just sat in the kitchen, his head hung over, teary-eyed and chain-smoking Lucky Strikes. Thank God, he was not a drinking man.

"Just remember, Ted, you gave them hope in their last hours. They left here happy and I bet were talking about their future plans, not feeling as bad as they had felt before," Mother told him. "I hope so, Monkey, I hope so. I just know they would have made it. The boy was turning things around. He wanted to make amends for his past. And she was right there with him," he said.

There were some lighter memories from his probation work. One evening I recall riding with him to nearby Johnston County to see one of his parolees, a famous bootlegger, named Percy Flowers, also known as the "king of the moonshiners." He was the friendliest guy you'd ever want to meet. His fame preceded him, since he had long been a kind of Robin Hood for his community. He was generous to hard-luck neighbors, even though he did not extend his benevolence to government tax collectors. Percy tried his best to give my father a country ham, but he politely refused.

I saw being honest by example that night. It is those kinds of lessons that stick, too, much better than a talking to. Plus, my dad was savvy enough not to turn the bootlegger in for trying to bribe him, because he knew that it was sometimes better to obey the "spirit," instead of the "letter" of the law. In short, he had the common sense to cut people some slack in life.

He grimaced as we drove away from the bootlegger's house, and said, "Boy, I would love to have that ham."

Despite the satisfaction he had from his probation work, my father continued to want to do more than merely survive. He worried about all of us, along with his many financial obligations. It all weighed heavily on him, especially, I believe, because he felt he ought to rise above the norm in business, just as he had in prior areas of his life. Incongruently, he had an English degree from Wake Forest University. He had been a high school teacher for a while back in Martin County, where he was raised. He had done this work before he met my mother near her home in Wilson, North Carolina, about the time of the outbreak of the Second World War. He went on to become a naval officer in the war, and had served in the South Pacific, seeing hard action in the liberation of the Mariana Islands. He was in charge of keeping the landing craft in good repair. So, he had to be frustrated to have risen so high, to have been seen as an up-and-comer, to have been so educated, so decorated, to now be reduced to spending all his time working two jobs or more to only eke out a bare living. In the end, all he could do was simply keep working, keep dreaming and keep smoking cigarettes, which he did in abundance. One look at his yellowed, nicotine stained fingers, attested to this fact.

My mother, however, was not used to this hand-to-mouth living, along with the unending responsibility of raising three small children. She reminded him daily of how far she had fallen to live with this failed "country boy," not to mention the resentment she felt toward him for "throwing away" the family money. She did not grow up rich, per se, but she did grow up with a rich appetite for the finer things in life.

Her father, John Edgar Winborne, unfortunately, had the same taste for high living, and despite struggling to make ends meet, seemed to find delight in indulging his only daughter if he could. Mister Winborne was a jolly man who purchased a new car every year, despite his modest means, never knew a stranger and was well liked by his neighbors. He seemed to try all kinds of work, including time spent as an undertaker, farmer, store clerk, and police officer.

Mildred's mother, Lillie High Winborne, tried to reign in her daughter, but her sweet and timid soul was no match for her strong-willed daughter, or her enabling husband. In short, Mildred had been thoroughly spoiled as a child and young adult, even during the great American Depression.

Ted and Mildred, at heart, always liked each other. In one memorable scene in the western film, *Shenandoah*, Jimmy Stewart playing the sage father with many sons and one daughter, advised a young man eager to be his son-in-law that he would never make it in marriage with his daughter if he only loved her, because for it to last he would have to like her, too. My dad would have passed that test because he truly liked my mom, for they always preferred each other's company to anybody else, I felt, and often had talks full of chuckles and intimacies, except when they were fighting. They were, deep down, always rooting for each other, even if they were in a stew about the particular roadblock in front of them. But when the road got rough, her natural reaction was to strike out; his to withdraw. No marriage of any duration is without its burdens. And so it was with my parents.

So, Ted plugged along for over five years in the probation field, along with taking on the heavy load of running the beach apartment house in 1959. He would often sit at our kitchen bar stool late into the night giving oral reports via a little green disc to his supervisor. I remember him breaking up his slow, steady monologue by saying "Period. Paragraph."

My father was not content to be a run-in-the-mill probation officer. He was used to having some rank where ever he had worked, so he naturally applied to be the director of the statewide probation department when the job became vacant, after only two years on the job as a field officer. He wrote long letters to the area state judges who had influence in the matter, and even wrote a three-page message to the governor of the state, Luther Hodges, in 1958 outlining in detail his qualifications and the reasons for selecting him over more experienced candidates.

His ambition would not be abated by his disappointments. He was the little engine that could. He deftly explained in his letter to Hodges why his slim resume in terms of inside service was the solution between those in disagreement between selecting a long-term employee or an outsider with no probation experience: "It seems that appointment of someone from inside with a length of service long enough to be familiar with the set up and short enough not to have become acquainted with or involved in this disagreement (opposition to either veteran insiders or total outsiders) would be a double psychological advantage." Ultimately, he was not chosen. He accepted the defeat graciously, keeping his disappointment to himself, as usual, and pressed on.

With the probation head job settled, he was freed up to concentrate on his current job and run the beach apartment house. He was finally able to get a transfer to Wilmington from Harnett County, which may the twin responsibilities doable. He was now able to be nearby, even while on the job, during our second summer at Wrightsville. This proximity helped him to stay on top of things. I didn't like him being so available, however, because he could now show up at unexpected times to find more things for me to do.

Saturday's, of course, was the busiest day of the week because that was when new guests would arrive. The length of stay was usually for a week; sometimes for two weeks. Selfishly, we tended to be irked if a guest was staying only for a night or two, for we had to do the same preparatory work for their occupancy, and then clean up after them, as the longer staying guests. Nevertheless, I was the bellhop, for want of a better title. When the guests would check in, I'd be there Johnny-on-the-spot to carry their luggage to their apartment. I soon figured out that guests from up North would pay decent tips, but not local people. So, I loved it when I heard a "foreign" accent and was at their command like a greedy little puppy.

My brothers, Teddy and Johnny, had more to do with the cleaning of the apartments than I did. This meant airing out of the mattresses, changing sheets, sweeping and mopping the floors and cleaning the refrigerator and the gas stove. Each apartment had tall windows with screens, since there was no air-conditioning. Thus, the floors—if not everything-- tended to get sandy and gritty. It took constant upkeep to keep the rooms habitable. My main job was to keep the smelly trash cans emptied. The gray metal cans had to be lined with newspaper. We didn't have plastic liners back then. My other assigned job was to get a bucket and go to the front porch ocean side and pick up cigarette butts that had been flipped over the rail. Stooping over in the red hot sand and digging out butts is the lowest job a kid can have, especially when many of the guests, often tipsy with drink, would be oblivious of me beneath them doing my housekeeping chores and would continue to toss out cigarette butts almost on top of my head.

The toll on our family that summer could have been worse than anyone would ever know. Unbeknownst to any member of my family, I almost drowned. My mishap happened late in the afternoon in August when I entered the ocean to summon my brother, Johnny, who was out frolicking with girls.

"Hey, Johnny, Dad wants your help in the office," I said. He looked at me as if he was thinking: *Just when I'm getting somewhere with these girls*. He shrugged and said his good-byes, but they were still messing around with him, splashing water on his head. He swatted the water back on them one last time. Glancing at me, Johnny resisted the urge to kill the messenger, and swam back to the shore.

I lingered on, since the girls were still around. In addition, the water was warm and inviting, so much that I was slow to realize I was being gradually pulled out to sea by the strong undercurrent. I was about chest deep, a little farther out than I liked, but I was also preoccupied with trying to keep up with the girls that Johnny had befriended. But then the girls decided to leave. I had drifted out past them by then. They both said good-bye and quickly caught a wave to carry them into shore. Still oblivious to my perilous situation, I was having jealous thoughts about how all the good looking girls, it seemed, were attracted to Teddy or Johnny, but never to me. *I wish I was older*, I thought. So, I was alone in deep water, with the sun going down and dusk coming on. It occurred to me at that moment that the life guard had been packing up his gear to leave for the day when I had entered the water, a portent of bad things to come, as it turned out.

Suddenly, I realized I was over my head. My toes could not reach bottom. This scared me. But I tried, simultaneously, to stay calm. I began to tread water and begin my swim back to shore. I kept at it for a long while, swimming as hard as I could, but I was making no progress. I realized, as well, that the end of the pier nearby was parallel to me. *What? I must be really far out.* I noticed I could barely see the outline of the ocean front cottages.

I gave up swimming and began treading water again. I had to hold my breath and go under three times, just to give my arms a rest. While under water I would curl up in a ball before going up again to resume my treading. At least ten or fifteen minutes had passed by since I had begun my futile efforts to get back to the shore. I knew I was in trouble. The idea I might drown swept through my mind, but I swept it out again, choosing to concentrate on staying afloat. Thank God, I was not panicking.

But I did begin to yell "help," as loud as I could. I had begun my screams for help as I began to go under water to keep my arms from giving out. I knew I could not keep this up but for so long. To make matters worse, I noticed I had drifted beyond the end of the pier. I could no longer see the beach or any cottages, just water everywhere. My arms were weakening. I had swallowed some salt water, despite trying to spit it out. Doubt was beginning to creep into my mind.

Many more minutes passed.

It was so quiet.

I called out again.

No response.

Then I heard a voice.

"Shut up!"

What? I thought, *'shut up?' I'm drowning and this guy is telling me to shut up?* I was mad now and peddling all the more, but I kept my mouth shut. *Maybe, he wants me to preserve my strength*, I thought. A pair of strong hands grabbed me and pulled me to a rubber raft. The Good Samaritan was a grown man, probably in his thirties. I recall that he was tanned and had stubble of a beard, which kept scratching me as he paddled us in—he above the raft and me below it, face-to-face with him. I was so glad to see him that I couldn't care less if he had a scratchy face. In no time, it seemed, he had paddled me into the surf and to safety. He helped me to sit down, since my legs were pretty wobbly. I thanked him profusely. I owed him my life, after all. But to my everlasting shame, I didn't ask his name. I was pretty rattled, after all. After he had determined I was okay, he simply walked away. I then returned to our apartment house.

Mother chided me for being late for supper. I didn't mind, though, because I felt lucky to alive. I washed up and joined the family at the table. They had just begun to eat. After finally getting a word in edge wise, I mentioned that I had almost drowned. The noise level stopped for a moment, and then everybody stared at me. "Yeah, right," Johnny said. "You look all right to me," Teddy chimed in. Then my mother began telling a story about something or other. So, nobody took me seriously. Everybody continued to talk at once, happy and preoccupied, while lustily eating the food.

I just let it go and decided I'd let Jesus know and give him thanks, since surely he knew about my plight, even if I couldn't convince anyone else that I had actually been in danger. I basically shrugged it off, not realizing until years later what a close call I'd had. But at that young age, not yet a teenager, I thought that my survival was simply the way life should be. But the worst was yet to come for us in regard to facing the fragility of life, and we would be tested even more to figure out why bad things happen to good people.

Just as the Malone family seemed to be living the idyllic life on an enchanted island, the dark specter of death would fall upon our fortunes. We thought we were transferring forever from our dull times in rural Harnett County to fun-filled times at Wrightsville and nearby Wilmington. Yet, two tumultuous events would make their mark on us: the first would slow us down and the second would stop us in our tracks.

The first event had to do with when my uncle and aunt came to visit us. He was a young man, the youngest of five brothers, and we adored him and his family. Boots was his nickname, and his wife, Iva, was a cute, long-legged young girl who was also a cousin of my mom. My mother, in fact, had introduced Iva to Boots several years before, and the match was one seemingly made in heaven. They had one small child, Phil, about two-years old at this time.

Uncle Boots was a favorite for me because he would simply spend time with me, doing stuff like teaching me card tricks or playing catch. My dad played catch with me only one time while we were at Wrightsville, and the rest of the time he was too busy, but Uncle Boots was always a kid at heart.

After staying up late learning card tricks from Uncle Boots, we had gotten off to a late start the next day. But the sky was clear and blue, no clouds, and the ocean was as calm as a lake, just gentle waves with skinny white caps lapping in. I noticed that Mother was taking a break and was relaxing on a lounge chair, having a drink with my uncle. They were laughing and making pleasant small talk. He had his chair inclined backwards, so that he was kind of looking up at her. I came by, and tapped him on the shoulder to ask him for a stick of gum. I had the idea I could use a piece of wet gum to pry out a coin I had found stuck between two wooden floor boards next door at the New Hanover Club.

"I'm sorry, son, but I don't have any gum," he said in his soft, slow Southern voice. Mom didn't have any gum, either. I said it was all right, and walked off, while they returned to their conversation. I did overhear her telling him he needed to get a checkup with the doctor as soon as he returned home from his visit with us. He nodded in agreement, while also rubbing his eyes with his fists. He was a little groggy, having just got up from a nap back in his apartment. I said bye and left.

I fiddled around for about fifteen minutes, giving up on getting the gum I needed. I circled around the New Hanover Club, which was next door to our apartment, and walked back to our place, returning from the front side, which faced the sound--the inland waterway separating the island from the mainland. I was entering the front door when I walked into what seemed like a house of horrors. First, I saw my mother's stricken face through the screen door.

"Don't let Charles in here! Oh, God!" she cried. She then ran down the hall to our apartment. I was perplexed, to say the least. I saw my grandmother, Nanny, who was visiting with us that week, walking erratically in another direction, all the while making cooing and mournful sounds, her arms waving, distraught.

What in the world! What is going on? I thought.

Then I saw the teenage girl who was babysitting for my aunt and uncle, little Phil in her arms, rushing toward me in her effort to get out through the front door. She brushed by me, her face contorted in shock, tears flowing down her cheeks. She said something about Boots, but I couldn't be sure exactly what she meant. So, in all the commotion, I just kept walking through the hallway toward the screen door that led to the front porch on the ocean side. Other people were running by me, not paying me any attention. *Something's really wrong on the front porch*, I thought. With increased anxiety, I opened the screen door and kept going to the location everyone else was running away from. At first, when I got to the side porch, everything looked normal: the sky sunny blue, clouds fluffy and white, the ocean sparkling and, beyond our porch, the beach teeming with scores of preoccupied vacationers, oblivious to the developing tragedy.

Then I rounded the corner to our wide front porch that directly faced the ocean, turned left and stopped in my tracks. There in a corner, still in his swimming trunks, flat on his back, was my uncle, and there was a guest I knew as Colonel Hamon, kneeling over him. He was slowly fanning my uncle's upturned face. I froze. My heart stood still. My throat went dry.

"Is he asleep?" I asked, as I got closer.

"No, son, he's dead," the colonel said. His blunt way of delivering the dreadful words had the implausible effect of calming me down.

I bent down over Uncle Boots to get a closer look. I still could not help trying to make futile talk to him, but his face and presence had a stillness I had never seen before. I knew he would not respond. If I had any doubts of his lifelessness, I was shocked into the gruesome reality of it when I saw a fly land on his forehead and slowly walk across it, bringing no reaction. I recoiled, staggered back and up into the colonel's reassuring arms.

This view of death was far away from what I was used to seeing, the kind seen in a decorated funeral home where the deceased is powdered up, embalmed and ready for display. No, this was unalloyed death, suddenly thrust on me. I then ran away from the grim scene on the front porch. I headed for my place of solace: Benny's room, next door.

It turned out that Uncle Boots had a massive heart attack. He could not be saved, despite there being two heart specialists there as guests. The two doctors were nearby and were able to administer to him almost immediately. My mother said she held his head while they tried to resuscitate him, even plunging a needle into his heart with drugs to revive him. But after a while, one of the doctors looked up to my mother and asked her if she knew the number of the local coroner. At that moment, she recalled later, she felt that she was going to faint.

Now, their next dreaded duty was to go upstairs and tell Aunt Iva, an excitable woman. The doctor went with Mildred to the second floor apartment where Uncle Boots and Aunt Iva were staying. Mother had warned the doctor to expect a highly emotional response. So, the doctor had a tranquilizer ready.

"We knocked on the door and she called for us to come in," Mother told later. "She was singing up a storm while she was frying shrimp on the stove.

"I entered with the doctor. She turned and smiled, but when she saw the doctor, she stepped back a bit. She asked, right off, 'Where's Boots?'

"I went to her and told her that Boots had died, as tenderly as I could, but she twisted away. She wanted to run downstairs. She then commenced to screaming. The doctor stepped in then and gave her a shot. That calmed her down, but she was a mess, poor thing. Telling her about Boots was the hardest thing I've ever had to do."

Our dad was away on this horrific day and had to be flagged down by the Highway Patrol somewhere in Harnett County. He was still working there during the weekdays.

Dad got back to us late that night. We gathered around and for the first, and only time in my life, I saw my father break down and shed tears. He was a disciplined man, a man of the South, a Naval officer, and he was not the type to break, but the death of his little brother was simply too much. His tears, of course, triggered ours and we were all balling our eyes out. To my child's eyes, seeing my daddy cry was scary to the bone. Uncle Boots' death cast a pall on our first, otherwise idyllic summer on Wrightsville Beach. It was a kind of warning shot across the bow that our time in this place would not be the utopia we envisioned. Of course, we intuitively knew that life is life, no matter where we are located. We were able to carry on with good cheer because we so wanted our new adventure to work out well.

15

Our second summer on Wrightsville Beach in 1960 was more of the same, much fun in the sun, surf and sea. We had no more tragedies or near drownings. But Dad was there every day, thanks to his transfer to Wilmington by the probation department. He was always around the corner, it seemed, and was able to more closely rein us in, and get more work out of us. Each week he would gather Teddy, Johnny and me in the office, critique our work and hand out a dollar for our efforts, or lack thereof. He was solemn about it, took his time, which gave the event an almost ceremonious air. But when he finally quit talking and handed us our pay, I felt proud, not to mention heartened to have my father, so often absorbed in his work, attend to me a little as he looked at me with his kind, yet careworn, face.

But we had big decisions to make that fall. My oldest brother was entering his senior year in high school. My parents decided it would be best for us to stay in Coats to let him finish there. My mother had been forced to move during the Depression years in the middle of her senior year in high school, away from her long-held friends, and she insisted the same fate would not befall her son. So, my father decided to stay the fall and winter alone on Wrightsville until the rest of the family could join him the next spring. The plan was to sell our home in Coats and purchase one in Wilmington. Mother could keep her job as attendance counselor for another school year. And Teddy would be able to finish school where he had started. It seemed a good compromise, but it did leave my father being left for long periods of time alone at Wrightsville. We were all so focused on our own school plans that I am afraid we gave less thought than we should have to how isolated he would be under these arrangements. He was so practical that we never imagined he might miss us and be lonesome.

The long spans of time away from our father began in the fall of 1960. We were back in Coats, trying to readjust to new shoes, long pants and shirts with collars. It was tough after being barefoot and wearing nothing but swim trunks all summer. We also felt distinctive, what with being the only kids in our little town who had avoided the tobacco fields and could brag that we had spent the summer working and living on the beach.

It was also this same fall that I began, for the first time, to get interested in politics. Everybody was a Democrat in those days, but it was a form of Southern Democrat left over from the Civil War and Reconstruction era of the 19th Century. Republicans were still persona non grata in the South. This was because they were the party of Lincoln and the ones who had defeated us in what we called the "War of Northern Aggression." The Democrats were still the status quo party in the South in 1960, reliably backing small business, opposing unions and blocking civil rights initiatives at every opportunity.

Yet, there were signs of change and John F. Kennedy, a liberal, in our eyes, had won the Democratic nomination, so it was a fiery time that fall, and a time of reconsideration for many old Democrats. Another "liberal" Democrat, Terry Sanford, was elected governor of North Carolina. Thus, the Democratic Party began taking baby steps towards being a progressive party, especially on racial issues, yet it remained the dominant party for North Carolina.

My father and mother were life time Democrats. I believe my father was pretty moderate; he was staying with the party even though Kennedy and Sanford and people of their ilk were leading the party, both from Raleigh and Washington. Governor Sanford did not lead North Carolina like Deep South Democrats, such as George Wallace of Alabama, who were continuing to defend the legacy of segregation of the races.

My father had some progressive ideas at that time on race. In the early 1950s, he had helped, as part of his duties as the county schools attendance officer and probation officer, to set up a home in Harnett County for "Black juvenile delinquents." He helped black leaders to raise private funds for the project.

The Dunn Dispatch on April 4, 1955, wrote: "The Black citizenry of Harnett is to be congratulated for carrying out this home project." Upon my father's resignation in September of 1955 to accept a job with Colonial Frozen Food Lockers in Dunn, he was credited in regard to the black home at Seminole "to being in large measure responsible for the establishment of the state's first privately endowed black delinquent home in Western Harnett County. Since the establishment of this home others like it have sprung up in several places." He received high praise for his reformist zeal, especially for black children, but the praise could not pay the bills. Fortunately, when my father transitioned to the private sector again, my mother was appointed to take his place as the county attendance officer. She did not inherit the probation part of his job, so those duties must have been transferred to the state.

So, our family had two incomes for the first time. We were not ahead of the game financially, but we were less behind than we had been. Since all three of us boys were in school, it was possible for my mother to be gone all day at a job. It was still a bit of a novelty for both parents to work outside the home, but it was a novelty that was dying fast.

My mother, who would go on and hold the job for seventeen years, retiring in 1968, was primarily in the business of keeping kids, both black and white, in school. She would travel throughout Harnett County, deep into the rural areas if need be, to check attendance records, and then she would visit the homes of the truant students to convince their parents, or whoever was their guardian, to return them to school. If a child was perpetually truant, he or she could be taken away from their home and put into a county juvenile home for children.

So, my mother was involved in working with teachers to build children up, not down, in order to motivate them to stay in school. I believe this work helped to nurture in her a benevolent attitude about the down and out. Her kindly ways for the poor were in contrast, however, to how she felt about her peers. She was proud of her self-commissioned aristocratic background and propped us up as a distinguished family, as if we were swans swimming among geese, despite our meager circumstances. I suppose Mother's charity of spirit toward the poor and blacks in those days had as much to do with her sense of noblesse oblige, as it did to actual liberal philosophy. Whatever the motivation, she organized efforts to bundle up clothes for the poor, and to deliver it, usually to black teachers, for distribution. My mother also worked in the summer, in later years, for Head Start, an anti-poverty program established under President Johnson to assist disadvantaged youth to prepare for school.

I also had the unique experience of hearing straight from the horse's mouth about how discrimination was so painful, and so illogical, for blacks. I was accompanying my mother on her attendance rounds one day. I must have been around ten or eleven years old, when she called on the principle, W. D. Porter, at a black high school near Lillington, called Shawtown.

Principal Porter was a kindly, distinguished man. As a black male rising in the public educational system controlled by whites, he had learned to be both strong and patient. I knew he was a persistent thorn in the side of the white leadership of the county school system, based on listening to my mother talk about him to my dad over supper at home. The superintendent, an old white fellow, considered Porter little more than an agitator because he was always nagging the powers that be to get adequate school supplies, reliable buses and undilapidated desks and chairs for the black schools. Usually, all the best stuff went to the white schools first. But Mr. Porter never let up. He and my mother shared a rare quality: they both wanted to be right over being liked. On this visit, we got to talking about how the local white-only greasy spoon, Wade's, was the target of a local black demonstration; the goal to desegregate the place. Mother and Mr. Porter were shaking their heads at the stupidity of public restaurants being segregated.

"Now, Mrs. Malone," he said calmly, "it is not that I want to eat at Wade's. I suppose the food there is the normal fare, certainly nothing better than I can get at home. But what makes me, and most all blacks, uncomfortable is that we are not allowed to go in there. The idea of being excluded is the rub. If I was allowed to eat there, frankly, I would probably choose not to. But going there or not would be my choice! Having the choice, not the food per se, is where the justice is!" he said earnestly. I thought I saw his eyes glistening. I felt embarrassed that he, a grown man and a school principal, to boot, was denied entry to a place that even a kid like me could go to, just because I was white.

"And also, let me tell you, and listen to this Charles, when I go on a trip from here to, say, Florida, with my wife and my young daughters, I have to plan it carefully."

"Why, Mr. Porter?" I asked.

"Because, child, those white gas stations that will fill up my car with gas will not let me or my family use their facilities to use the bathroom or to go inside to get a Coke or something to eat."

"Really?" I said. I was aware of this in a vague sense, but hearing about his plight first hand had my full attention.

"Yes. We have to know where the places are in-route that will accept blacks. We have to plan accordingly on any long-distance journey we make."

"But everybody gets thirsty and has to go to the bathroom!" I exclaimed.

"Exactly," Mr. Porter said quietly.

"But, ah, Mr. Porter, you are a principal of a school," I said, taken aback at the thought that this esteemed man would be denied entry anywhere. Mother and Mr. Porter both were looking at me at me in unison, both seemingly embarrassed to reveal to me that the adult world was so badly flawed. I believed, as well, that he felt it was more important to enlighten me than to hide any shame he felt, despite being a principal of a school, because of his subservient position in life.

I learned a lot that day. I learned that society was not always fair, by a long shot. I felt Mr. Porter's pain, and that feeling struck home much more than any eloquent sermon on social justice would have for me at that young and impressionable age.

I also had an unlikely mentor in my home county in regard to doing the right thing during an epochal day in our nation's history: the assassination of President John F. Kennedy on November 22, 1963.

It happened this way.

As we entered my sophomore year at Coats High School that fall our awareness of national politics and world events was expanding. I was taking American history and civics and was expected to know things beyond the confines of Harnett County. This was no problem for me, however, as I had developed a keen interest in politics. I certainly was a fan of our new president, John F. Kennedy. The Kennedy family was super stars, and their attraction went beyond partisan politics. We had only dim memories of Eisenhower, who was a grandfatherly figure, unlike the dynamic and youthful Jack Kennedy and his high-flying brothers and sisters.

I was sitting in a civics class on a Friday, around noon, on November 22, listening to my teacher, Miss Frazier, drone on and on, when I noticed the principal, J. C. Hawley, standing at the open door. He waved at Miss Frazier to come to him. They began an animated conversation right there in the hallway. This was a little unusual because the principal usually called on the intercom if he wanted to see a teacher. Classes in progress were not casually interrupted. So, we were all staring at our teacher and the principal, wondering what was up.

But then I heard something that was unbelievable.

"The president's been shot," he said.

"President Kennedy?" she asked, as her hand went to her mouth in alarm.

"Yes, and it's bad, I hear."

"Oh, my God," she gasped.

We began exchanging wide-eyed looks at each

other. The vile message was rapidly being repeated. We were all beginning to talk now. Some kids didn't believe it; others were terrified. Then we heard people walking up and down the hall, more talk, and the din of dismayed voices picking up. Kids poured out of the classrooms. Several girls began to cry. The teachers were also upset; control was vanishing. Within the hour, Mr. Hawley ordered all students and teachers to gather in the auditorium. We were in the process of getting to the auditorium when we got official word over the radio that the president was dead. Some of us, unfortunately, were getting updates by word-of-mouth. I was in a state of shock. I was thinking, *how could our president, so young and exciting, be dead? No, this cannot be!*

When we got to the ground floor hallway to enter the auditorium, there was one rough neck kid horsing around, laughing. He said something like, "Good riddance."

At the moment the kid said those blasphemous words, old J. C. Hawley walked up, grabbed the kid, and pinned him against the wall. He yelled at him to shut up and be respectful of everybody else's sorrow, if not his own. The kid shut up. He knew better than to lock horns with the principal, who was in his face in a big way. Back in those days the kid wouldn't have thought about filing a brutality suit against the principal, for authority asserting itself was the norm, while students acting out was not. We all glared at the recalcitrant red neck, now stiffly getting line. He knew then to keep quiet, or he would have his tail whipped for good. I would have been happy to lend a hand.

Not to make little of our principal's fine talk to us during the assembly, where he wisely brought us together to explain the tragedy as best he could, but I will never forget how he put that kid in place with a moral and physical force that matched the intensity and shock of that traumatic day. I was proud of J. C. Hawley. It was his finest hour.

16

My time in Saigon began to take on a routine as the months went by. I had to remind myself that most the GIs in town who got killed were those who became lax, thinking rear guard duty was like being at home. We had a blotter full of street crime that happened each night, much of it done to our troops who were in the wrong place at the wrong time, usually full of beer or high on something. We had to stick to the beaten path, so to speak, not wander off into civilian neighborhoods, often teeming with resentful natives more than ready to get revenge on the Yankee invaders. So, I pressed on and made sure I drove the van on my currier runs with all the skill I could on the crazy, crowded, blighted roads. I knew better than get into a road incident with any native, for the local police would never find me, an American soldier, as anything but guilty. It seemed our enemies wanted us dead by all means necessary, while our so called allies wanted us dead, too, but their weapon, by necessity, was one by a thousand cuts.

I got through this particular day without a hitch, fending off beggars when I had to make a quick stop near the American Embassy downtown, and then had a smooth time on a brief run with the command sergeant major who wanted to make an unannounced visit to a bar on Du Do Street where he liked to catch soldiers lounging during working hours, hoping the dark, smoky backrooms and loud jukeboxes and bar maids would protect them. The last face they expected to see was our big old tough as leather face of Sergeant Wilson. The big guy liked to do routine patrol work now and then, just to keep in practice. In this case, he got the lost soldier's attention and cut him a big break by telling him he had thirty minutes to get back to his post, or he would be a guest in our detention center. But my mind was still on home. My reverie the night before about my home and family while leaning on the ledge of our billet under the starry night made me want to return there and start up where I had left off.

I wanted to think about the worst day of my life. The fall of 1960 was mainly taken up with high school life for my older brothers. Johnny was a sophomore and showing great promise on the athletic field. Teddy and I would always hustle to play the best we could, but Johnny was a natural. My father used to pay Teddy one dollar for each point he scored in a varsity basketball game, but he raised a white flag of surrender when Johnny scored fourteen points in the first game he played in. My sports career was budding, but still contained to seventh grade level competition. But all of us boys were head over heel in school activities of some sort. But even with a busy school schedule, it was hard to ignore the red-hot political campaigns of that fall. I made the first political speech of my life when I was chosen to make a presentation on behalf of John Kennedy to our seventh grade class, while another student made a pitch for Richard Nixon. Kennedy won in our straw vote.

So, we were glued to the TV set on election night, November 8, 1960, to await the results. The voting returns were slow to come in, however, so Johnny gave up and went to bed early. That left Teddy, Mother and me to look on. But we were drifting off to do this and that as the night progressed.

My father had been away for a couple of weeks. I suppose he may have voted that day, if he had registered in Wilmington. I never found out, but I suspect he was too wrapped up in making repairs on the apartment house to bother voting on that day. He was especially busy at that time with fixing and upgrading the gas stoves. We had gotten a nice call from him the weekend before the Tuesday night vote, and he'd told us he had a surprise for us. The weekend before our mother had been at the apartment house with him, a rare outing for them without us. He had taken her to see a house he wanted to purchase. He and Mother had decided we would have a separate home in Wilmington from our personal apartment at our apartment house. They enjoyed their time together without us boys demanding their attention so much.

The historic election night, as it turned out, would leave us forever transformed, but not because of politics. The phone rang around ten o'clock, which was a little late for a call. I heard the ring from the kitchen, where I was sorting my socks out of the laundry hamper. Teddy was with Mother in the living room where they were watching television. The phone was in there, so she answered it. She listened to the message for several seconds and then let out a scream. I heard the commotion and came running down the hall to see what the matter was.

"Ted is dead! Ted is dead! On, no. Oh, my God!" she cried. She kept repeating this grotesque announcement, as she slapped her feet to the floor and pounded her fist on the table.

Teddy looked at me. I looked at him. We were speechless and too shocked to do anything but stare at our mother as she writhed in agony.

Mother was going berserk. Teddy was trying to comfort her until the doctor arrived. Somehow, she had summoned up the wherewithal to call him. I rushed upstairs to tell Johnny.

"Johnny, wake up! Daddy is dead!" I blurted out. I shook him awake with no thought to what I was doing, or how I was hurting him.

"Who's Daddy?" he answered, not fully comprehending my ungodly words that had broken his sleep. "Our Daddy! Get up!" He ran downstairs to see the emotional bedlam that was unfolding in the living room. When he began to comprehend everything, he became angry, hitting the back of the couch, vowing to ever work hard and be a son his father would have been proud of. Teddy and I had little to say. Within the hour, the house was full of friends and neighbors. In a small town, word travels fast and my dad was a popular guy in town. He was only 45 years old.

My mother took to bed, distraught. She was under close scrutiny for 24-hours. We boys were sent off to a neighbor's home to ease the crowding and turmoil under our roof.

My father died of a massive heart attack that struck while he was in the middle of upgrading the apartment cooking stoves. He was handing some wire to a couple of guys through a hole in the floor, when he suddenly collapsed. When he didn't respond to their calls, they scrambled out of the crawl space to see what was wrong. They found him lying on the floor, already dead, a Lucky Strike smoldering in his hand.

The next three days were a blur of frantic and mournful activity, ranging from being corralled into the funeral home for the open casket viewing, to sitting on the front row at the crowd-packed funeral at the local Baptist Church. We were on parade, under stress and bewildered. At the age of thirteen, a bazaar side bar to grief when your daddy dies is to also have feelings of embarrassment from everyone staring at you, pitying you. When I returned to school a couple of days after the funeral, I was humiliated when my teacher told me in front of my fellow students to "be sure and bring an excuse for being absent this week!" I wanted to crawl in a hole because I knew all eyes were boring in on me; I was the kid with no daddy anymore.

But there was another despicable thing that happened during our time of mourning, just before the funeral, that did bring on a sense of mortification for us as a family. When the news of my father's death reached the African American educational community, they were both shocked and aggrieved. My father had been a supporter of theirs at a time when it was hard for blacks to have a white friend with any influence with the powers that be. My mother was also well regarded for her truancy work, which included the black schools in the county.

So, it was only natural that a small group of black teachers, including Principal Porter, would want to get together and come to our house to pay their respects. And they did. They parked their car in our backyard, amid the cluster of other cars there, and proceeded cautiously, certainly respectfully, to our back door. The house was full of people, many who had brought cover dishes to tide us over during the troubles. There were other visitors standing around outside. Nobody was giving the group any trouble at this point. But they had the misfortune to be met at the door by a relative of ours, whose racial attitudes left a lot to be desired, and he ordered them off the property. I heard they did not protest, still expressed their condolences, and left with the same dignity with which they had arrived.

The African American group made no effort to come to the funeral after the humiliation they had endured at our home. My mother, later on, said had she known that they were outside; she would have asked them in. She said they would have been welcomed. The crazy thing about this episode is that my uncle was in so many respects, other than in how he felt about blacks, an ace of a guy.

But I was beginning to learn at an early age that my white elders, good as they could be otherwise, often cast a blind eye to the black community when it came to fair play and human decency. Even the most benign in the white community thought the definition of a bigot was one who dislikes blacks more than necessary. I was beginning to become resentful about this dreadful paradox, because I had learned a simple lesson from Sunday school, a lesson from a Christian child's prayer, which I had taken to heart, even if my white elders had not, which read:

Jesus loves the little children,

All the children of the world,
Red, yellow, black or white,
They are all precious in his sight,
Jesus loves the little children of the world.

Anytime there is an unexpected, tragic death, like that of my father, each day afterwards for weeks is busy, as well as emotionally draining. There are hundreds of things to be done, or to be endured. We did all of those things, but after a while, the mourners drifted away, the calls quit coming in, and we had to pick up our lives as everybody else was doing. When I could finally catch my breath, emotionally speaking, I had my first big cry about a month after my father had died. I had been feeling guilty about letting my dad leave our house without us telling him good-bye as we should have. We boys had been playing basketball in the neighboring yard, when Mother called to us to come and say good-bye to Dad. He was standing by the car, ready to return to Wilmington for the work week. They both waved to us. We ran to the fence that separated us from our back yard, about 100 feet away, waved good-bye to him, and then returned to our game. We should have jumped the fence, run to him and given him a hug. She said he said, "Well, I guess they're more interested in basketball than me." He looked hurt and then left.

She scolded us for not returning to our yard to give him a descent good-bye. I wrote him a note of apology, at her command. A few weeks later, when we had to part again—for the last time— I was thankful I had given him a good handshake and smile. I couldn't hug him because I was wedged in between my brothers in the back seat of our car. He had been driving, but handed over the driving chores to my mother because he was joining up with a fellow probation officer to ride with him to Wilmington. We were taking another route to our home in Coats. All of that guilt was flooding in my mind. Mother held me closely, rubbing my head, as I wept uncontrollably. She was ready, at last, to be strong for us.

The loss of a parent gone too soon is a loss that hits a child from the inside out, not the other way around. On the surface, we were okay. The tragedy of it, in the ensuring years, was that he was not there for us. His influence was secondary. We did a lot of stuff he would have said no to, but since he was not there, we went on our merry way, having no reason to doubt our own judgment since there was nobody to stop us. Our mother, to be frank, was a pushover for letting us get our way. We didn't know the errors of our ways until years later, and only then could we see that we had only been drifting, more often than not, instead of building up our lives. In the meantime, however, we thought we had it made. Mildred had long resented the "smother love" of her mother, our Nanny, who lived up the street from us in Coats. Our saving grace, however, was that we were devoted to the memory of our father, and any mention by our mother of what he would have thought of us, gave us pause before we did anything too harmful. His memory was a barrier, but one with many holes in it; we still did not always live up to his example. But by the loss of our father, we were thrown into a new reality: we had to sell our beach apartment and stay in Coats. It made sense because we simply couldn't run the place without Dad. Our mother didn't want to be there without him. She hadn't liked it that much when he was alive.

We owed money on the apartment house, to boot. It burned my mother up that she had to pay about $5000 to rid herself of the obligation to make payments on the property. It might have been worse if we had not had my father's good friend, Robert Morgan, a local lawyer—who would later be elected state attorney general and a United States senator—handle our estate free of charge. And the final reason to stay in Coats was that Mother still had her full-time truancy officer job. So, we were back in our little country town, no longer feeling special, and no longer being treated special. We were on our own in much reduced circumstances.

17

The most popular way weary G.I.s found relief from the war in Vietnam was not from chasing bar girls and visiting bordellos, it was music. Besides having stereos, cassette recorders and radio, there were live bands all over the place. One of our hotel billets booked bands—usually from Thailand or Australia-- on occasion-- for performances. They did okay, whereas the local Vietnamese bands were not too good. I have to say they tried hard to copy Western pop and rock, but listening to familiar songs put to the Asian interpretation was often downright comical or pathetic. Yet, we still showed up for the rock impersonators because it was still nice to relax and be entertained, if for nothing else, to forget our troubles or fight off loneliness for a while.

Then I heard about the Vietnamese C.B.C. Band.

"This band is unbelievable," my friend, George, from California told me. George was a rocker wannabe, so I figured he knew what he was talking about when it came to bands. I listened up.

"Let me tell you guys, this chick lead singer is like Janice Joplin. She can belt out all the shit I like to hear, like Grateful Dead, Santana, Beatles or whatever."

Well, that was enough for me. I was tired of the Asian groups I'd heard so far, even though I appreciated their good intentions, if not ability, to perform American and British rock and rhythm and blues. But the good word on the C.B.C. band had piqued my interest, to say the least.

"One other thing," George continued. "Look out if you go. The Cong hates them. They blew the C.B.C. club to smithereens one night not long ago. I heard the blast went off right in the middle of them doing 'Purple Haze'." *They tried to do Jimi Hendrix? Impressive,*

George, warming up to his subject, said excitedly, "Yeah, the place was packed with Americans, too. I think a couple of people, including one G.I., bought the farm, you know, died that night. But they are back now and playing somewhere else."

"No way," I said. I was really intrigued now.

"Frickin' A. Hey, there's more: one time their lead guitar player—and, get this, he wears his hair down to his waist, really cool—he is walking down the street, right, and some Commie stabs him in the chest, yelling that he was for traditional Vietnamese culture."

"Wow!" I said, transfixed now.

"Yeah, he survived, thank God." George got up to leave. He turned at the door and said, "Man, they're the best. What's more, these kids love it. They ain't faking it like those shitty Vietnamese bands we hear at the U.S.O. Go see for yourself." By now, I was mesmerized. I had to go see them.

Within a few days, I went in search of the band. It was risky to see them, for they played in a club downtown—named The Ritz Club-- that was largely unprotected. I knew going to a club with live music, far from the safety of an American military base was suspect. Such places were magnets for illicit behavior, especially drugs. I knew trouble could break out at anytime, but I was ready to take my chances. I wasn't tempted by drugs, and the available beer was standard fare. If Charlie (word for Communist guerrilla fighter) would leave us alone, I expected to be fine. I was determined to see this band.

I found my way to the downtown club, at last. It was named the Fillmore Far East. The name of the club was a take on the classic rock venue on 2nd Avenue in the East Village in New York City. It was also referred to as the Ritz. It was inconspicuous, except for the guard at the entrance. Being in uniform, I was waved in without ceremony. I walked up the stairs and passed through a beaded doorway. I entered a dark room whose walls were covered with aluminum wrap. It was gaudy looking, but the stage looked well stocked with the standard array of musical instruments and sound system. There were a few red, blue and yellow lights strung around to give the place a party feel.

My nostrils took a hit from the sweet weed being smoked, in competition with the rank smell of regular cigarettes. This ambiance was not so different from clubs back home, so I felt comfortable enough. The place was packed with soldiers all wearing fatigues, many of them well into their beer or weed. I got a beer. I found my seat and settled in for the show.

The lead singer was a petite Vietnamese girl named Bich Loan, who had a smoky voice that defied her small stature. She covered both great male and female rock singers, such as Janice Joplin or Jimi Hendrix. The band did strong renditions of songs like "Higher and Higher" by Sly and the Family Stones, "Freedom" by Jimi Hendrix, "I'm Your Captain" by Grand Funk Railroad and "War Pigs" by Black Sabbath.

The lead guitar player was named Tung Ling, who was nimble enough to do the intricate sounds necessary for these rock classics. His great guitar play simply blew us away. Marie Louise, a sister in the family and later married to Tung, sang the softer, or folk, songs and provided backup. Her shy, gentle performance style was popular and perfectly fit for her song selections. The bass player and the drummer, their siblings, were first-rate. What got me was that

George was right: they seemed to love doing Western music. It was not phony. The C.B.C. was family, literally, with cousins and brothers and sisters making up the whole group. They took the look of Western hippies by wearing their hair long, putting on sunglasses and wearing floppy hats.

I was transfixed by the great music, the counterculture atmosphere and the joy emanating from everybody there. I wound up seeing the C.B.C. Band several times downtown. By early 1972, they had a gig at the Tonsunut Air Force Base, so I figured that was a promotion for them, a kind of grand acceptance by the American brass that they could do justice, and then some, to American music. Yet, even though they were on a finer stage at the military facility, the C.B.C. had seemed almost exotic in their own secretive, dark, smoky club. We had felt hip, even radical in a vicarious way, to be in their hideaway separated, if only for a few hours, from the harsh world of war outside. Many G.I.s, including me, would say in years to come, that going to see this band was the perfect antidote to the stress of being away from home. I was relieved to hear that these kids made it out of Vietnam when the country fell to the Communists in 1975. I shudder to think what would have become of them.

I usually listened to the likes of James Taylor and Carole King, so I was sowing my wild oats, musically speaking, to see the C.B.C. But anti-war rock and such was growing in popularity in Vietnam by 1971. By this time, the popular pro-war song from 1966, "The Ballad of the Green Berets" by SSgt Barry Sadler was in the musical dustbin with the hordes of disillusioned soldiers in Vietnam. They wanted songs that let them voice their anger at the war, not support for it.

The musical menu went from intense songs like "War, What is it Good for" by Edwin Starr, and "Paranoid" by Black Sabbath, to the soul-searching songs that spoke for peace in a gentle vein, such as "Imagine" by John Lennon, "Where Have All the Flowers Gone" by Peter, Paul and Mary and "What's Going On" by Marvin Gaye. Popular songs that touched our lovesick hearts were "Brown Eyed Girl" by Van Morrison, "Somebody to Love" by Jefferson Airplane and "Light My Fire" by the Doors. If we didn't have our cassettes or albums, we usually heard our music from the American Forces Vietnam network broadcasts, which was played all over Vietnam from the Delta to the DMZ. The AFVN deejays, such as the great Adrian Cronauer, kept our morale up with great distinction. Cronauer was later made famous by Robin Williams in the film *Good Morning Vietnam.*

The thing that always struck home for us was hearing live music. It was a rare treat to hear good music in person. That is why such bands as the gutsy C.B.C. were so appealing to us. Great cover bands, come to think of it, were paying American music a compliment, since it is generally acknowledged that imitation is the highest form of flattery.

18

A cherished benefit the military gave each of its soldiers in Vietnam was a five-day Rest and Relaxation (R&R) vacation out of country during the one-year deployment. We all looked forward to this diversion from our daily grind in-country. When I was there we had pretty exotic choices, such as Australia, Hawaii, Hong Kong, Thailand, and Taiwan. My first choice was Hong Kong and my last choice was Australia. The former because it was glamorous and affordable, and the latter because I was tired of the boorish behavior of Aussies I'd seen in Saigon bars. If there was a bar fight, count on an Aussie to be in it. The most vicious bar fight I ever saw was between two Aussies. They both were drunk and one of them had fallen to his knees. The other guy then took a step backwards, set himself, and swung his boot forward, kicking the guy on his knees in the face, splitting his nose up the middle. The blood gushed out like a geyser. The rest of us scattered, not wanting to be drawn into this wild fray.

Lots of Australian bands came to play for the troops, so a lot of their soldiers showed up. I was prejudiced and, if I had it to do over again, looking at the Aussies from a broader perspective, I would have visited there.

So, at the last moment, and because Hong Kong had been scratched off the list, I chose to visit the island of Taiwan. I went with my old friend, Jim, my MP friend whom I'd seen my first day in Saigon.

Taiwan lies just off the coast of mainland China. After the end of World War II, the Chinese Civil War resumed between the Chinese Nationalists, led by Chiang Kai-shek, and the Chinese Communist Party, led by Mao Zedong. By 1949, a series of Chinese Communist offensives led to the defeat of the Nationalist army, and the Communists founded the People's Republic of China on October 1 of that year.

In December 1949, Chiang evacuated his government to Taiwan and made Taipei, to his mind, the temporary capital of the Republic of China. Many of China's intellectual and business elites evacuated from mainland China to Taiwan, as well. Old Chiang Kai-shek was still in charge when we arrived there for R&R. We were hoping to see him, but I realized after I got there that public access to him was impossible. He was an exalted figure, not available to the people as Western political leaders routinely are.

The thing about this beautiful island that captured our attention was the contrast between these Asian people at relative peace as opposed to the Asian people of Vietnam ground down in war. We saw genuinely nice people and well-kept lawns and streets and buildings. We saw affluence and modernity—including hot water for the first time in months—and though we saw poverty, it was more in the rural areas and not spread everywhere, on every corner, as it was in Saigon. We happened to be in Taipei when the island was celebrating its independence day (actually celebrating the overthrow of an ancient dynasty in 1912 on mainland China—but the Taiwan government under Chiang considered itself the real Chinese republic, not the Communists under Mao; an ancient conflict I will not fully explore in this story).

Festivities included a big military display, along with many aspects of traditional Chinese and/or Taiwanese culture, such as the lion dance and drum teams. There were huge crowds lining the streets in anticipation of a parade. I was astonished to see the police freely and casually beat back the people with their wooden batons. The people, to my equal astonishment, didn't seem to mind, or to be surprised by the harsh tactics of the police. But I will tell you this: the streets were cleared quickly and thoroughly, and the parade was able to commence in its grandeur without the people getting in the way.

Ironically, the special guest for the parade, representing the United States, was the then governor of California, Ronald Reagan. I had also seen him back in Wilmington, North Carolina, in 1959, when he was the grand marshal of the annual Azalea Festival there. The old actor had come a long way since his days as a pitchman for Borax. And little did I realize how much further he would go in the future. I felt comforted by him being there, however, even if our politics did not jell. I still had pride as an American that he was representing my country.

The trip was a true respite from the hustle-and-bustle of Saigon. I had a suit tailor made for about twenty-five dollars—a steal. When we attended a variety show nightclub act, which included singers, dancers, trapeze artists and animal acts, I was struck by the large number of wealthy looking Asian businessmen with beautiful ladies, many dressed in brightly colored kimonos, on their arms. I doubt that many of them were their wives. The Asian conviction, I have read, that what goes on during the morning in the office and what goes on during the evening behind closed doors bear no relationship to one another. But who was I to judge since my friend, Jim, and I were accompanied by charming escorts of our own. Having female escorts available was a service of the hotel. I hadn't been in my room for five minutes before a bellhop knocked on my door and kindly let me know I could have my pick from a stable of ladies, as it were. These girls were akin to the Japanese geishas, not their lower class counterparts: prostitutes. It was not done in a cheap or degrading way, and there was no indication that the escorts—who were lavishly turned out— had to do anything amiss beyond keeping us company.

We also made a long trip to the northern coast to see the China Sea. We were able to make the one-hour trip by taxi—another sign of how cheap things were-- and how we were relatively rich as American soldiers, compared to the native people. The northern coast was remote and rural; most of the villages were hamlets, sort of like the shanties we saw thrown up in the worst areas of Saigon. The coastal road wound between the hills and the rocky shore along what is known as the Jumping Stone Coast, from the days before the road was built when travelers along the north of the island had to jump from rock to rock. We got there and roamed the rocky, mushroom like shapes of the rugged shoreline. We marveled at the huge crashing waves that met the rocks, letting up a gigantic spray that fanned up and over the perimeter.

An enterprising young Chinese woman, a local, followed us around taking photos.

"Go away, please, we don't want pictures!" I said. She laughed and took more. "You need pictures. Good for you." She tilted her cone straw had back a bit, and ran ahead of us to photograph us from another angle.

I got tired of saying no, and wound up posing for

her, as if it was a professional photo shoot. Later, we met with her and argued furiously, and with great glee, to haggle her down to an acceptable price for the negatives. Our session around the table drew a small crowd, all who clapped and cheered when we finally made a deal. I still treasure the photos we got that day. But just as we were getting used to the sane and peaceful life away from Vietnam, so enhanced by the sweet and kind people there, it was time to fly back to the hot, crass, busy streets of Saigon. But the time away had its curative effect, and we returned with refreshed bodies and minds. We also got to see the appealing side of oriental culture, a culture able to flower when unencumbered by the ravages of war.

19

In the fall of 1969, more than 500,000 people marched on Washington to protest U.S. involvement in the Vietnam War. It remains the largest political rally in the nation's history, according to *Time Magazine* reports from that era. The demonstration, titled the Moratorium to End the War in Vietnam, was the first large demonstration against President Nixon, who was in his first year in office, but still carrying on Johnson's policy to win the war militarily. Large-scale rallies such as the Moratorium were noticed by the American soldiers in Vietnam. Yet, the soldiers did not see protests as the cause of our stalemate there, but as the result of it. The North Vietnamese had already figured any war of attrition, which had been U.S. Commander William Westmoreland's approach, would play into their hands. They had always been prepared to fight for twenty years or more and to give up ten of their soldiers for every one of ours, and, in their mind, still win, according to passages accredited to their leader, Ho Chi Minh, and their military ground leaders.

The Asian way of thinking, as opposed to the Western way of thinking, seemed to be on display by our different approaches to the Vietnam War. The Asian mind sees intelligence, or being smart, evidenced by the way one struggles to get the right answer, even in the classroom, while in the West, being smart is evidenced by how quickly one can find the answer. For us, the more the struggle, the less intelligent one is seen to be. In our classrooms, the pupil who is last is considered a laggard, even if this pupil, who has shown more diligence and perseverance than his quicker counterparts, finally achieves the right answer. For us, the student who struggles the least is seen as the brightest.

This flaw, or difference, to put it kindly, was illustrative in the patience shown by the native Vietnamese to stay the course in the war, as opposed to Americans, or the Vietnamese heavily influenced by the West, who were impatient and saw the obstacles to victory as valid reasons to withdraw from the conflict, or to fight halfheartedly. In this, we never understood the oriental mind. We thought they would surely give up after x and y and z had happened to them, but such setbacks never deterred them, not at all.

Our protests were a natural confirmation of how the American public would act after so long a time at war and after so many thousands of casualties. Our soldiers began to act out, not take orders, and committed violence on their military leaders by "fragging" them to avoid going into combat. There was a rapid increase of drug use, including heroin and marijuana. Racial tension was building up as black soldiers were questioning why they had to bear the brunt of the sacrifice, especially when they felt they fared much more poorly back home than whites. The social unrest building up was a simultaneous one: by Americans at home and in Vietnam.

American soldiers had a right to be indignant, if for no other reason than the fact that the people we were defending— the South Vietnamese— didn't want to win as much as we did. The South Vietnamese Army wouldn't fight worth a damn. The political leadership was corrupt to the core. The esteemed president of South Vietnam, Thieu, for example, owned a hotel in Saigon that was the site of a well-known bordello. We're supposed to "do or die" for this guy?

To add insult to injury, we could tell the rural population in Vietnam was sympathetic to the Cong, not because of communism, but because they felt they were people indigenous to them, who were the true nationalist. The common folks over there saw our Vietnamese supporters—the Saigon crowd—as frenchified collaborators with foreigners.

And our soldiers saw the South Vietnamese Army and the Saigon regime being mostly interested in having Americans do the dirty work for them so they could stay in power, make money and never be at risk. It was well known if one looked around Saigon that the draft age young men of the prosperous were not serving in their own Army. Their military exemption schemes were similar to our own in America. The adage rang true in Vietnam, just like at home: "It's an old man's war, but a young man's fight."

There were calls to end the Saigon corruption, such as Lt. Col. John Paul Vann, who died in Viet Nam in 1972 when he was working as a civilian in the pacification program following an influential military career. He wrote a book called *A Bright Shining Lie*, wherein he tried to expose the "incompetence and venality of the South Vietnamese Army." Vann always thought America could win the war if she would fight it the right way and do right by the Vietnamese peasantry rather than just for the their rich leaders, who were mostly Catholic with French connections from the French Colonial days. Vann advocated winning the hearts and minds of the common people in Vietnam, as the Communists were doing, by ending the Saigon corruption and called for the "American millions getting down to the poor instead of being siphoned into the feeding trough of the Saigon hogs." Unfortunately, Lt. Col. Vann, a North Carolina native, got scant attention from Washington. I began to perceive the negative reaction to the American presence late in my tour after two incidents.

Firstly, one evening when I was off duty I had decided to go with a fellow soldier to a restaurant downtown. We had barely begun our meal when there was a huge explosion. The side wall partially caved in and the lights went out. There was smoke everywhere. We were all knocked to the floor. We were not hurt, but were stunned by the blast. My ears were ringing, but I scrambled to my feet and headed for the front door. The blast was the result of dynamite, or some explosive device, that had been thrown into the place directly next door by a guerrilla fighter driving by on a scooter. Seventeen people were killed, I heard. I saw a few on my way out. In particular, I saw a man who was on the ground, writhing in pain, who looked like he'd been cut a thousand times, blood covering him from head to toe. I saw a woman lying in a pool of blood next to a cab, obviously dead. Sirens were blaring, people were screaming and MPs were quickly on the scene with guns drawn. I couldn't do much, since I was off-duty and was not armed. We were not issued weapons unless we were on a designated mission, not when we were frequenting taverns or bars in the entertainment areas of the city. I would have preferred to be armed at all times, but we had to go by the rules. The Vietnamese police eventually arrived, as well. We stayed around to be of any help we could, but were told by our MPs to get back to our billets. We did just that. Again, the front lines were everywhere, and this incident was proof of that grim fact.

Secondly, I had decided, naively, to walk away from the close surroundings I normally walked in, when I wasn't performing the occasional jeep patrol, and visit Saigon University. I knew the school was only a few blocks off the beaten path I was accustomed to. I was breaking my rule about beaten paths, but my curiosity got the best of me. I successfully made my way to the entrance of the university when I first caught sight of some students. It was my hope to have a dialog with the young, idealistic Vietnamese who were not on the take for the Yankee Dollar. I was in uniform, however, another mistake that proved provocative to the students when they caught sight of me. They slowly rose and, in a fit of agitation, began to wave their arms, raise their voices, and walk down the steps toward me. Their faces literally had looks "that could kill."

"Di di mau!" One kid yelled.

I knew that meant to get the hell out of there right now. I came to a halt on the front sidewalk. The students were making their way in my direction. I had seen enough. I turned around and started making tracks away from the approaching danger. But the students began chasing me. I picked up speed and ran as hard as I could go. Thank God, I was slender and quick. It took me three blocks to lose them, but I did.

I was shocked by the student's reaction to me, or, at

least, to what I represented in my American uniform. And I was shocked that it was South Vietnamese students who had rejected me. I knew then that the Vietnamese friendship I had been experiencing was nothing more than noblesse oblige. The intellectuals there hated us, I now knew. I also understood that the common people, the peasants, had to resent us, as well. Our only friends in South Vietnamese were those making money off us in some form or fashion. In my despair, I thought: *What are we doing here?*

My impromptu visit to Saigon University coincided with what was a tense time for us in Saigon in the fall of 1971. This was when South Vietnamese President Nguyen Van Thieu ran for re-election. We were on an emergency footing. I was required to carry an extra pistol and M-16 on my courier routes through the city. I know I was driving with extra precaution during the campaign time. A story from *Time Magazine* entitled "South Vietnam: The No-Contest," set the stage by describing President Thieu as a man acting like a candidate we would expect to see in the West, but that the contest was a "no-contest," since his was the only name on the ballot. Thieu's confidence for his re-election was well founded. According to a *Time Magazine* article, Thieu had Nixon's promise that the United States would continue to support him and his authoritarian policies. The article also revealed that the U. S. Embassy had sent word among South Vietnamese military generals that any attempts to overthrow Thieu would end American assistance. Thieu was well prepared to face any opposition at home, the article continued, by having his police forces positioned throughout Saigon to stop any protests against him, including blocking off Saigon University, a known site for dissidents and protest activity. And to think I thought I could traipse around Saigon University in full American trooper regalia.

Another historic event in 1971 that further eroded support for America's engagement in Vietnam was the publication of the Pentagon Papers— an expose of secret and deceptive United States actions that led to its involvement in the war. The papers were assembled by a large group of researchers. One of the research leaders was a top-level defense analyst, Daniel Ellsberg, who had decided that the war was wrong, and he believed that the information in the Pentagon Papers should be more widely available. He handed over copies of the papers to the *New York Times*, then the *Washington Post*. News writers from those newspapers put together stories from the purloined information and published them in June of 1971.

The released report, called The Pentagon Papers, created a political bombshell. The essence of the story by the *New York Times* said that the American people had been lied to by the U.S. Government for the past twenty-five years. The publication was shocking to the public. The expansion into genuine warfare began, the *Times* summarized, "despite the judgment of the government's intelligence community that the measures would not cause Hanoi to cease its support of the Vietcong insurgency in the South...The bombing was deemed militarily ineffective within a few months." The *Times* further revealed that the American government persisted in Vietnam primarily to avoid "a humiliating U.S. defeat" rather than to free the Vietnamese people. President Johnson is on record saying he would be damned if "he'd be the first American president to lose a war." So, our national leaders' vanities was the likely mover and shaker behind our long stay in Vietnam, even if it had to be satisfied by the blood, sweat and tears of American soldiers and their families.

We had access to Time Magazine in Vietnam. When it reported bad news, such as The Pentagon Papers, it was not redacted, for our benefit. I usually bought a copy off a newsstand at our billet. I recall reading about the contents of The Pentagon Papers, once discussing it with one of our officers over coffee.

"I can't believe Johnson wants us to sacrifice like this just because he is too proud to lose," the captain said.

"Yeah. The big boys say we can't win, even with our bombing," I said.

"We'll just have to hold on and cover our own ass."

"Captain, I follow you. We'll look after each other."

"You got it, Malone."

So, we pressed on, but it was heavy lifting emotionally when we knew, based on our own publications, that we were there with no winning strategy in sight. No end game. The releasing of the Pentagon Papers played a key role to ignite the flames of an already flaming anti-war movement at home, and this turmoil certainly added to the frustrations of the ground troops in Vietnam, further intensifying the breakdown in discipline and to the loss of purpose. I could tell, even in my modest position while in Vietnam, that our military leadership was losing confidence in our mission. We'd talk among ourselves, such as I had with the captain and with officers present, about why we were still fighting the war in such a protracted and aimless way, and nobody could figure out why we continued to dig the hole deeper, except for the vanity of our own American leadership.

America's loss of purpose in Vietnam not only affected our broad policies, but also seeped down to pollute the mindset of the everyday soldier who still had a job to do, whether they liked it or not. I was on the receiving end of this slackening attitude when I was once again assigned to guard duty. The normal shift was about five hours, as I recall, and after that time a replacement would come on to relieve the first guard. On this evening I had worked all day since seven o'clock in the morning and anticipated doing my guard assignment from 8 o'clock in the evening until one o'clock in the morning. Things were going well, until I had to warn a lone man staggering up the street, which turned out to be a lost, drunken American merchant marine, to get off the street. He was breaking the curfew. I quickly hustled him to an abandoned room and told him to sleep it off and I'd get him up later. I was going to tell my replacement about the merchant marine, but at one o'clock nobody showed up. I couldn't leave my post, so I simply stayed on. My ability to stay awake began to falter as the hour's drug on. I struggled to stay awake until the second shift ended at 7 o'clock in the morning. I was able to get the sotted old merchant marine out of his room and out to his ship without any trouble, but when I was finally relieved, I struggled to keep my senses to go directly into work, as I was scheduled to do.

I was fuming over nobody showing up. We may have all developed a lackadaisical attitude about our duties, but it was still highly dangerous to put any soldier in danger by leaving him exposed, especially when that soldier had not prepared himself with enough sleep beforehand to pull an all-nighter. I reported the incident to the powers that be, but to my amazement, nothing much happened. A few months later I heard a sergeant, a draftee named Bill, I believe, who was set to return to the United States in a few days, joking about how he had stiffed some guy on guard duty. I heard enough to know that the guy he had stiffed was me. I walked up to him, angry.

"Let me tell you something, Sergeant, that guy you stood up was me." I stepped closer and eyed him sternly. "I didn't appreciate it then and I don't now."

"It was you?"

"Yeah, me."

Bill had always been disagreeable to me. He was a smug Ivy League guy heading for law school. He wore his superiority on his sleeve. He now rolled his eyes and looked to our staff sergeant for help. He had a look of exasperation, certainly not of contrition. But the staff sergeant just stared at him, doing nothing. Bill was on his own.

"I don't think you were the worst for it," he said. "Why should I risk my neck with only a few weeks to go in this shit hole?" Then he looked away from me, shifting his attention back to his deskwork.

"Just because you don't like the war and you're ready to go home doesn't mean you put somebody else in danger," I said, my voice rising.

"Well, sorry," he said. He was now simply uncomfortable and irritated. His body may have been in Saigon, but his mind and heart had already lifted their wheels for the flight home.

"Okay, Bill, hope you have a fine career back home. You should do great. I'm sure you'll screw over anybody you can to get ahead."

"Leave it be, Charlie. I'm getting tired of this conversation," he said, now shuffling his papers and getting up to leave.

I stepped in his path and said quietly, "I'm not leaving it alone, you asshole. I'm turning you in." Then I stepped aside, as he scurried from the room.

Which I did, but to my knowledge, Bill went unpunished and got to go home to what I supposed would be a prosperous career. He should have been brought up on charges, but the MP brass just let it go. They didn't want to bother with it in the waning days of the war. But to me, honor was honor, and watching each other's back was our duty until the last day and last hour we were there together. I felt if the ground troops in the jungles could do their jobs under the most dangerous of conditions, we in Saigon should do ours, as well. It wasn't just a matter of me having to put in unwarranted overtime; it was much more than that.

The Army core values we were taught in basic training—values I thought were hokum at the time—loyalty, honor, respect, selfless service, and courage were what a soldier was all about. I had thought everything about the military was less than honorable when I was first drafted, but now I knew that the Army and other branches of government had to do what the civilian leadership told it to do, for good or ill. I knew individual officers had to do what they were told to do, even if they disagreed. But the one thing that had to be adhered to was fidelity among the soldiers on the ground. Now, I felt the sting of every-man-for-himself that had replaced the Army motto to look after each other. I wanted out of Vietnam as much as anybody, but I was still going to be a soldier as best I could. I suppose those devils in basic training had drummed a little of the Army spirit in me, after all.

20

Although I was learning to be a standup guy in regard to helping my fellow soldier, I still had enough rebel in me to want to have my say, probably more than I was supposed to have. One day a fellow soldier brought around a petition he was seeking signatures for to protest Nixon's decision to bomb inside the boundaries of Cambodia, the neighboring country.

The North Vietnamese had been launching offensives against American forces from their sanctuaries in Cambodia for some time. So, President Nixon approved a plan to bomb Cambodia in hopes of destroying the North Vietnamese bases hidden in the Cambodian jungles. However, Nixon knew that if they chose this route and it leaked to the public, the national protest against war in this expanding form would grow worse. So, he decided to keep it secret from the American public. Nixon never consulted Congress and even kept the bombings a secret from high-ranking officials in the military, some reports said. But the bombings became public soon enough in the spring and summer of 1971 and the uproar began, including with many in the military. Anyway, when the petition was put in front of me, I signed it without giving it a lot of thought, as did a few other guys.

The petition drive, unfortunately, did not go unnoticed by our command sergeant major. The next day CSM Wilson called us few who had signed the petition into his office. We gathered in front of him, scared stiff. He stood up from behind his desk and slowly looked us over, breaking into a slight grin, but his eyes were peering into us like bores. He picked up a piece of paper and waved it slowly before us.

"Now, who in the hell decided to send around this petition," he asked.

"Ah, I did CSM Wilson, and just a few of us signed it," the guy from California said. I, for once, had not instigated the situation at hand.

"Well, you guys must be the stupidest bunch I've ever seen. I can't believe the names I see signed on this damn thing." He looked at Ricky, a real Okie from Oklahoma, not your usual anti-war type.

"Ricky, you signed this? You?" Wilson said with an air of incongruity.

"Well, I just signed it to be sociable. So, I could get

back to my work," Ricky said, rather unconvincingly.

"I guess that is the stupidest answer I've ever heard." Wilson said. "First, you don't know if bombing in Cambodia is smart or not; and second, claiming you wanted to get back to work is hard to believe." *Ouch*, I thought, *got him with both barrels.*

Then he looked me in the eye, too.

"And you, Charles, I know you're a thoughtful guy, but this is one you should have thought about a lot more," he said. To see a man you admire look at you with disappointment written all over his face is a rebuke hard to take.

"Fellows, I can't believe this petition in the first place. Soldiers are here to fight, to serve, not to protest. When you get home, protest all you want. But not while you are in uniform. I could throw you all in the brig, by God!" He stopped to gather himself.

"And I can't believe you men would do this to me, right in the Provost Marshal's Office. I can see some grunts doing this, even if it's wrong, but not you desk jockeys."

We were all feeling the heat by now. I glanced at the instigator of the petition with a fierce look that said, *what were you thinking?*

"Here is the deal, men," he said, now lowering his voice to barely a whisper, "I am obliged to turn this petition over to the Provost Marshal, then he can deal with you according to the Code of Military Justice. Or I can do you a favor, and me a favor, and tear this rag up. We can forget this ever happened and go back to work. What say you?"

We looked at each other, all of us scared and feeling the shame of letting CSM Wilson down. This man had helped us all throughout our tour. He had been tough, but fair. We realized our petition would make him look bad. We also knew the petition would go nowhere up military channels. We knew the Cambodia bombing was technically illegal, but we had little sense if it was an effective policy or not. But if we signed petitions for every SNAFU in the Army (Situation Normal All Fucked Up) we would be signing petitions 24/7.

We looked at Wilson and shook our heads in collective agreement, signaling him to tear up the petition. He was only too willing to do so, right in front of us, to boot. As he let the scraps of the paper fall into the trash can, we all just went back to work.

I learned there was a time and place for everything. We felt it was not fair to make our Command Sergeant Major suffer when the end result of our action would have done little more than assuage our own egos by protesting. Sometimes, we have the ability to do something, and have the opportunity to do it, but then see that perhaps we shouldn't do it. I think this was one of those times.

That evening we were sitting around the billet talking about CSM Wilson. We were all white guys, but we still admired the big man, who was much closer to us than the two officers in the detachment. The officers, one the colonel and provost marshal, and the other a lieutenant colonel and deputy provost marshal, seemed far removed from our daily routine. The hierarchy was top to bottom, for sure. But we admired how Wilson made us want to do right, not by coercion, but by his example. He was tough, but fair. He was by the book, but he knew when to bend it now and then. He made us forget he was a man of color, no small feat for 1972.

"I'll tell you what, the old man saved us today," Ricky said.

"Don't you know it," I said.

We were relieved that the whole spectacle was over. We decided we'd stay clear of signing any petitions, no matter appealing they might be. "Hey, let's get a beer someplace," one of guys, Joe, from Brooklyn, said in his very Brooklyn accent.

"Sounds good," said Steve, who had suddenly walked up to join our little group.

"Who invited you, Steve," Joe said. Steve was a stickler for doing everything by the book. He was a nerdy, bespectacled guy, who didn't look like the Rambo type he styled himself to be. At least, I knew what I wasn't.

"I'll add a little class to the group," he said, trying to be funny in his awkward way.

"Yeah, right, Steve. Dress up all you want," Brooklyn said grinning. "You're so ugly that you'll never need birth control... your face will do just fine."

Steve turned red, glared at Joe, who stood up to face him down, the grin wiped off his face. Steve stepped back, swallowed hard, trying to settle himself.

"Well, if you don't want me to go, fine by me," Steve said. "Besides, you guys look as disheveled as the soldier I just saw going by on the street."

"Disheveled, big word," I said with a chuckle.

"I just don't see why soldiers, or sailors, can't look good in uniform."

This was enough for Brooklyn.

"You ever thought that this guy, this shitty looking, uh, disheveled soldier, may have just survived hell on earth in the boonies? He probably killed some Cong or just missed getting killed. Could be his buddies did get killed, so now he is just hanging on. The last thing he needs is a prick like you hassling him over his appearance," Brooklyn said, again staring hard at Steve, his fists balled up tight.

"Joe's right. If the brass lays off them, then we sure as hell should," I said. "Heck, I barely salute our detachment officers, anymore. We forget about it when we're working together all the time."

"Suit yourself," Steve stiffed. "I didn't want to go out tonight, anyway." We all laughed.

It was confusing sometimes to know when to be military-like and when to be casual. The war atmosphere made military formalities seem petty, especially in a war footing, even in the rear guard areas where due diligence was still necessary to keep safe.

At that point, Steve, all huffy like, got up and left. Some folks never see the gray areas in life. The military brass did, to their credit, let up some on the spit and polish in Vietnam.

But not entirely.

I got sloppy one day late in my tour. I met a fresh lieutenant on a path somewhere near MACV (Military Assistance Command—Vietnam) and failed to salute him. He reamed me out much like CSM Wilson had the officer who failed to return his salute months back. I was tired and full of my own thoughts when we came upon each other, was not trying to be disrespectful, but the damage had been done. I took his lengthy rebuke in silence, gave him a sharp salute and went on. *Oh, how self-important you think you are, and us in the middle of a real war, not a damn parade ground*, I thought. But still, I regretted not showing common courtesy to an officer I was not on a familiar basis with. I had gotten over bothering with petty displays of disrespect that I once thought I had to do to stay real.

.

21

At long last, my time in Vietnam was dwindling down to a few days. Our tours were set for a year and then home we went. During the war years at their height, the reserves were never activated, so hundreds of thousands of guys avoided having to serve overseas that way. I don't doubt some folks chose the reserves for the right reasons, but many joined to stay safe. Other folks who preferred to not visit Vietnam opted for extended stays in college, marriage and family, jail or fleeing to Canada. Young people facing the plight of being drafted widely and openly discuss the various ways and means of avoiding the draft. The guys that wound up in Vietnam tended to be those with the least means or smarts to get out of it.

If one was hot to trot to get to Vietnam, the doors were wide open for them to take part. However, fewer and fewer took that option, as the popularity of the war had plummeted at home by the time I got there. None were craftier in figuring out how to stay out of harm's way than the future chicken hawks, neoconservatives and other ferocious noncombatants who would in the future have no problem pushing other people besides themselves—or their own kids—into the wars in Iraq and Afghanistan.

Heck, I made it into the Army reserves myself. The problem was I got my acceptance letter in my third week of Basic Training in the regular Army. I knew my goose was cooked, but I took my acceptance papers to the company sergeant, anyway. It got a good laugh.

But now, I felt good because I was almost done with it all. It looked like I'd get an early out, as well, which meant I would complete my full obligation of 24-months in just 21 months. The Army thinking was that re-assigning me for three months after I got home from Vietnam wasn't worth it, so I could get my walking papers in Oakland once I returned. Processing time there was two days max. *Hot damn!*

It was still tough to say good-bye to friends I'd made in Saigon, including the Vietnamese staff I was around. I grew to adore the locals who worked in our detachment. They were humble and hard working. The females wore traditional long dresses called "ao dai" meaning "flowing tunic," always demure.

I felt the Vietnamese women in our hire had little respect for the often tawdry Vietnamese girls hustling drinks in the bar areas of town. But the disrespect among Vietnamese was relative, since the secretaries were looked down on, as well, by the Vietnamese population estranged from any role with the omnipresent Americans in the country. I heard there was a local law prohibiting any Vietnamese woman from walking with an American on the streets, lest she be arrested by the Saigon police for prostitution. Their thinking was: what else would a self-respecting Vietnamese woman be doing on the street with the "ugly Americans."

The Vietnamese locals needed us, but they didn't like us, it would be safe to say. To the common Vietnamese, not the elite, we were simply uninvited guests in their country, which bewildered us since we were not there for our health, either. What we didn't pick up on right away was that the South Vietnamese working class, certainly the poor, resented us because they knew their miserable condition would not likely change no matter who ruled them. I had one of our Vietnamese employees at the detachment, a middle-age gentleman we only knew as "Mr. Thieu" tell me to my face that Vietnam would be better off when Americans went home. He said it kindly, emphasizing he meant no personal offense. I was slightly offended at the time, but knew in my heart that it was true. Mr. Thieu knew he was doing well, had made his choice.

He was speaking about his many compatriots who had not thrown in their lot with Americans. He felt that Vietnam had to rely on her own people, not outsiders, to survive for the long haul. He also didn't want the French, Chinese or the Russians around either. I was surprised, for I felt he was just another Vietnamese parasite living the good life off of us, and who had no regard to the general welfare of the country. He probably didn't, but was just being honest with me. Or I may have awakened him too quickly from his daily afternoon nap, whereby he groggily said the truth before his feigned loyalty kicked in.

On my last day at work, one of the female secretaries ran out to my van, as I was getting ready to drive away. Her name was Lien. She was beautiful, long black hair down to her waist, her figure like an hourglass, and at that moment, for the first time, her misty eyes met mine. Her soft hands grasped mine.

"Oh, Charlie, I'm glad I see you before you drive away," she said, catching her breath.

"Thanks, Lien. Nice of you to come out here under the hot sun."

"No matter, the sun." She hesitated and smiled, still holding my hands. "I miss you. You always so nice."

"So kind of you to say that, Lien." I kept looking at her, as if I'd never seen her before. I could feel a slow burn, but it was too late now.

"Lien, I've got to go. You take care, now."

"Okay, Charlie. Bye-bye."

We both knew we would never see each other again. I thought at that moment, in a flash, of how I wished I had gotten to know her better. But I never tried to romance the traditional women, certainly not those on staff. It almost always turned out badly, for them in particular. Yet, I felt a stab of pain in my heart to leave her, a young woman I barely knew, and a young woman whose future had to be a doubtful one. All of these thoughts swirled through my mind, but I had to let go of her hands, give her a last smile, and leave. As I drove away, I will always remember her standing there, so beautiful and so fragile. She stood alone on the dusty road. She gently waved to me as her figure grew smaller and smaller. I never saw her again.

As I thought of all my friends and colleagues, I knew our time had not always been heroic, but neither had it been wasted. I had gone from a green kid who was afraid of the traffic when I first arrived to a steady courier who could drive as crazy as the next man on the wild streets of Saigon. I pulled guard duty when called and stood ready to defend my brother soldiers, if need be. I simply did the jobs assigned to me. I was no hero, but I had pulled my weight. I was the everyman draftee, I suppose, whose story was unremarkable, mostly ignored by chroniclers of the complete Vietnam War experience.

I worried about the Vietnamese who would be left behind. I knew we all would be gone before much longer, no matter how the tide of the war was going.

America was already in the process of getting out of Vietnam, come what may. Between us and our Vietnamese allies, our exit strategy was the big elephant in the room.

There were many brave and kind people in South Vietnam, certainly in Saigon, who had put their lives and fortunes on the line to be allies with America. I didn't consider the global politics of it all when I thought of the people close to me. For them, it was mostly survival, not allegiance to our politics. We often ignored that distinction and felt the Vietnamese serving us believed just like us. Some did, of course, and there were some true South Vietnamese patriots who wanted a democratic state and a wider freedom, but I hate to say, there were fewer of these people than those who merely wanted to be one nation, no matter the governance.

I finally packed up and was driven by van to the same base where I had entered Vietnam: Long Bien. It was still a spread out air base, but had a rural feeling after being in the compactness of Saigon. I could breathe, at least, since the air was cleaner, if nothing else. I remember my last night out in Vietnam was spent at a little base bar, which was packed with American soldiers, few Vietnamese, for a change. Some of the guys were new, but most had been around for a while. By now, I was tired of male talk in general. Listening to a loud jukebox near my seat, I noticed a hot new song called *American Pie* by Don McLean. It spoke of home for me.

After a couple of nights on base, we were shifted to Bien Hoa Air Base for the flight home. The route home would take us on a southern swing through the Pacific, with stops at Guam and Hawaii, before arriving in Oakland. But first, we had to get off Vietnam in one piece. We were all worried about standing on the tarmac, because we'd heard stories about the Viet Cong lobbing in mortars that had killed departing soldiers, who had been standing in the wide open, vulnerable as sitting ducks. Pretty cruel, I thought, to get killed on the last day of a tour.

We were herded out on the tarmac, getting our last dose of the dry, hot air. I scanned the tree line and wondered if anything dangerous would yet zoom in on us. We were all nervously looking around, itching to get out of this unprotected area and onto the plane. Even on board, we were anxious to see the wheels lift off as soon as possible. But our last formation went fine. The Boeing 707—our Freedom Bird—was a beautiful sight. We got in line and quickly filed into it. I strapped myself in, got a seat by a window and stared out at the flat and dry plains around me. I could see, for the last time, the rivers and broad, green rice patties and the scattered huts and the few wondering water buffalo. My last sight was of a few fishing boats, junks and sampans slowing making their way on the sparkling blue-green waters around the coastline.

As the outside view slowly transitioned from land

and trees to sea and sky, mostly white clouds, the pilot announced we were officially out of Vietnam air space. A roar of approval erupted. We cheered, clapped and did a few cat calls, but then settled down. I leaned back in my seat and gave a long sigh of relief. I looked around and all the guys were quiet now. Everybody seemed ready to settle in for the long flight. It would be several hours before we made our first stop, Guam. Our second stop would be Hawaii— American soil, at last! And then it was on to the California coast.

We knew we were damned lucky to be returning in one piece. We were subdued, not by relief alone, but by our memories of friends and colleagues left behind. We couldn't help but wonder what would happen to them. I know I said a prayer of thanks for my own survival. And I prayed for those who had come to a bad end in Vietnam. I knew I'd drawn the long straw by being rear guard. I figured some combat vets would have a certain contempt for my contribution, even if they didn't show it, but most would understand it took us all to run the war. Who made it and who didn't had little to do with getting what we deserved. The fates of war are always so capricious, when all was said and done. The fires of my resentment upon entering the Army had, at long last, been exchanged for a light of new understanding and empathy for everyone caught up in the cataclysm of the Vietnam War. Why should I have ever expected to be spared the full measure of what life can be?

22

After about five hours in the air, roughly 2,450 miles (3940 km), we landed in Guam, a tiny, but strategic island, in the South Pacific. It occurred to me that my dad had visited this same island in July of 1944 under much worse conditions than I was going through 28 years hence. He was part of the Navy landing craft squad that put the U. S. marines on shore for the fierce battle at that time between the Americans and the Japanese, who held the island, a U. S. Territory and the largest island in a string of islands known as the Mariana Islands. Liberation Day continues to be held on Guam to commemorate the 1944 battle.

I was impressed; several years after my time on Guam, as I went over his WWII letters to my mother that the letters postmarked close to July of 1944 never mention his perilous experience there. Not that he would have spelled it out, but nothing was there, even implicitly. You'd never know he'd seen any action apart from his boring, routine tasks he was assigned to carry out aboard ship, according to his messages home. He showed remarkable discipline, surely.

But the thrill for me on Guam was being able to wash my hands in hot water! I had not had this luxury since I was in Taipei. It was a small thing, but a significant sign I was returning to normal conditions. Our time was so swift on Guam that I saw nothing except the airport. We were back into the air before I knew it. We then flew for several more hours until we landed in Hawaii. Again, we had little time to see anything, just an hour, as I recall. So, I rushed outside and walked around until I saw a palm tree waving gently in the breeze. I stood and stared at it, taking in at least a sliver of the island ambience. Soon, we were up and away again.

After several more hours, we landed at the Oakland International Airport. We were back on the mainland at last. It felt like a dream, but it was real and my time away from home was over

It took me a few days of red tape to get out of the Army. The so called "physical" was done in mere minutes. At last, I walked up to the paymaster and drew my final check. I had a duffle bag containing a few civilian clothes, odds and ends, plus a pair of combat boots. I was wearing my dress green uniform.

I can't believe this. I'm out, at last, I thought, as I stuffed the pay proceeds in my pocket.

I was alone when I left the processing facility in Oakland, bound for nearby San Francisco for a few more days before I took a flight home to North Carolina. I remember walking through the door of the processing facility and out to the sidewalk. I was technically a civilian now, I supposed. I looked around, soaking up the mild weather, so less hot than it had been in Vietnam on its coolest day. It was bewildering.

After being around people constantly in Vietnam, it was disconcerting being truly alone, but I was determined to be happy in my new freedom. I was surprised I had such mixed feelings, was missing my Vietnamese cohorts and my Army buddies. We had all been thrown together for so long. I felt adrift, even among the lovely Spanish buildings and the lush California landscape. I had become a civilian again, the status I thought was more important than anything. But I had been thinking of only myself back then. I had changed since those early days as a green draftee. I thought of people besides myself now. I cared about how my compatriots were faring. My heart felt heavier, but I didn't mind, because I knew it was carrying the extra care for others besides me.

A few days later I had a wonderful reunion with my family. My mother, grandmother and my brother, Ted, were there to greet me at the Raleigh-Durham Airport. We hugged, laughed and cried, just overjoyed at our long awaited reunion. We held on to each other as we walked through the crowded terminal. I saw a few passengers in military uniform making their way through, usually alone or with a small group of family or friends. It was the norm then for returnees from Vietnam to straggle in on their own, drip-drip like. There were no parades, for sure.

We drove from the airport across Wake County to see my brother John and his wife Janine at their home in nearby Zebulon. I recall being unnerved at riding in the car going much over the 35 mph. I had grown accustomed to in the crowded streets of Saigon. As we drove along, again my mind shifted back to the alien world I had so recently left behind.

What had it all been about? I thought.

My query was not simply a throw away thought. I began to think about not only my own experience while in South Vietnam, but of the experience of our country—the United States—in this benighted country. In my rather comfortable life, I'd never had to contemplate the nature of war seriously. War had only been an abstraction to me. Yet, even in my envious assignment to Saigon, rather than to the killing fields of the jungles, I had experienced a taste of the fear, of the turmoil, and of the misery inside the sphere of a warring society.

In the end, America lost the war in Vietnam. Was it our pride? Was it our greed? Was it our tactical mistakes? Was it our decision to fight in alien jungles?

Was it quitting too soon? Was it our corrupt allies? Was it really a global communist threat? Who knows?

"Victory has a thousand fathers, but defeat is an orphan," John F. Kennedy once said.

Regardless, war, however it ends, is done on the back of the everyday soldier, airman, marine and sailor. The people who start wars for the glory or the profits or the power, should get in the back of the line when it comes to handing out medals.

But I was one of the lucky ones. I got home, finished college, and found in Donna Hamilton, the love of my life. We were married in Raleigh two years after I returned from Vietnam, in 1974, in a lovely ceremony at St. Michael's Episcopal Church in Raleigh. Donna was radiant as she walked down the aisle to the heralding sounds of Handel's water music. In ten years we would have a son, David.

Race and war had been defining events for me. I had my regrets, but I was also happy that I was brave more than I was afraid, smart more than I was dumb, kind more than selfish and, in the end, luckier than could have been the case.

We begin at home. For me, it was on the shores of Wrightsville Beach in the dark of night, in the halls of my high school, and on the teeming streets of Saigon. If we can't change history, it may be enough to simply change ourselves. In the end, we make our mark in the world as best we can, usually under the constraints of our poor circumstances.

In 1953, my father, in remarks given to a group of Harnett County school teachers, quoted Ralph Waldo Emerson when he said: "What lies behind us and what lies before us are tiny matters compared to what lies within us." Nothing in his star-crossed life made my father doubt those words, so how could I do less.

My tale is of an ordinary young man with ordinary ability, adequate courage, and a desire to be a good man like his father was. I climbed out of a provincial world, aided by the example of others, and grew to have a life of inclusion, of purpose and of love. My growth was not measured by money or power, but by what was inside me. The story of my life could have been one of mostly regrets, but, instead, it became a story of coming of age.

ABOUT THE AUTHOR

Charles Malone is a native of North Carolina. He grew up in Harnett County and lived two summers on Wrightsville Beach, where his family managed an apartment house. He served in the U.S. Army, including a tour in South Vietnam assigned to the Provost Marshall's Office in Saigon (Ho Chi Minh City). He managed a home improvement company, was a newspaper editor and writer, ran for Congress, and worked in the public human resources field for many years. He is a graduate of Campbell University. He lives in Raleigh with his wife Donna.

Made in the USA
Charleston, SC
15 February 2017